THE

TRUE CHRISTIAN,

EXEMPLIFIED

IN A SERIES OF ADDRESSES

FROM A

PASTOR TO HIS OWN PEOPLE.

BY JOHN ANGELL JAMES,

AUTHOR OF "ANXIOUS INQUIRER AFTER SALVATION—"YOUNG MAN FROM HOME"—"CHRISTIAN PROFESSOR," ETC., ETC

NEW YORK.
ROBERT CARTER & BROTHERS,
530 BROADWAY.

1858.

INTRODUCTION

THE celebrated COTTON MATHER, so distinguished for his systematic usefulness, was accustomed, almost at every entry in his diary, to insert in connexion with the letters G. D. (good devised), some useful project which he intended forthwith to put in execution. Under date of April 5, 1712, we find the following:—

"G. D. I have thoughts of publishing a book of *Pastoral Desires*, expressing the desirable things which a faithful minister will wish to see among his people. There may be many good consequences of such an action."

At a subsequent time the following was written:—

"G. D. My book of *Pastoral Desires* is now got through the press; and now, with many and ardent cries to the glorious Lord for his assistance, I will set myself to visit all the families of my numerous flock; and with all possible solemnity dispense the suitable admonitions of piety unto all sorts of persons in them; and then leave the book in each of the families, with my request, that every person therein may peruse it, and partake of his own portion in it."

This venerable man displayed great practical wisdom, as well as benevolence of heart, in his habit of recording every useful project, and afterward putting it to the test of experiment. A good thought should never be lost. Dr. Franklin acknowledged his great obligations to one of the little essays which this distinguished preacher and pastor prepared for his own people.

The author of the following pastoral addresses has fallen upon a similar method of doing good. It strikes us as peculiarly beautiful and appropriate. An occasional address from a pastor to his own people upon any one of the great topics of practical religion, must have its advantages over any other tract however excellent. It is like a letter from a friend, and is adapted to produce happy and indelible impressions.

When Dr. Payson was dead, and his remains were carried to the church, where he had so frequently and faithfully dispensed the word of life, his weeping people saw a paper lying on his motionless breast, placed there at his own request, with this inscription: "Remember the words which I spake unto you while I was yet with you." How could any withstand the touching appeal! A short address, rich with truth, and warm with affection, occasionally distributed among a people by their pastor, may be read and remembered by them when his voice is silent, and his form has mouldered back to dust.

The following addresses, as we are informed by

Mr. James, were never intended for publication, but having been found to be useful to his own church, they were, in accordance with repeated requests, given to the public, and have met with an extensive circulation in Great Britain. The topics discussed are practical; their spirit evangelical; the style simple; and manner affectionate. We see not why the pastors of large churches cannot imitate the plan to advantage. Why should not the press be subsidized, in aid of the pastoral work, as well as the pulpit?

W. A.

New York,

CONTENTS.

PASTORAL ADDRESSES.

No. I.

THE INCREASED HOLINESS OF THE CHURCH

My Dear Brethren: Grace, mercy, and peace, be with you, from God the Father, and our Lord Jesus Christ.

You cannot have forgotten, that, on the first sabbath morning of January, when discoursing to you from 1 John v. 14, 15, and showing you from this scripture, the rule and encouragement of prayer, I proposed to you a subject, with much solicitation and earnestness, as an appropriate matter of supplication for the present year: that subject was, *the increased holiness of the church.* Through the sovereign mercy of God, and the outpouring of his Spirit upon the preaching of the gospel, and the administration of religious ordinances among us, we are now become a large community, amounting nearly to eight hundred members; a fearful as well as joyful number for me to consider, when I recollect that for the care of each one of these immortal souls, I am to give account in the day of final judgment. How much do I need, and how urgently do I solicit, your prayers, that I may obtain grace to be faithful, and the supply of the Spirit through our Lord Jesus Christ.

You have heard me declare, that, although it is not my intention to relax in any efforts for the conviction and conversion of the impenitent and unbelieving, yet is my purpose, as God shall assist me by his grace, to labor more carefully for the edification, consolation, and spiritual improvement, of those who through grace have believed.

The magnitude of the church, instead of diminishing, greatly augments my concern for its internal spiritual state; since the greater in bulk a body becomes, whether it be a natural or moral one, the greater is the necessity of looking well to its healthy and prosperous condition. God is my witness, that I am desirous, not only of a *large* church, but of a *holy* one. He that follows us all into the closet of private prayer, and seeth in secret, knows how devoutly, fervently, and constantly I say, "Lord give me a holy church." What is the addition of numbers, without the increase of piety? It is only like the influx to a nation of a multitude of inhabitants, without any loyalty or patriotism in their hearts; or like the swelling of a body with diseased flesh.

This, then, is the subject of prayer, which I have already from the pulpit, and now from the press, propose as the peculiar matter of your solicitations for the present year, so far as they regard the church — *its increased holiness.* In submitting such a subject for your consideration and adoption, I do not intend to insinuate that you are, in this respect, below the standard of other churches of your *own* denomination, or the average of *other* denominations; or even below your own former state: no, but I *do* intend to say, that neither you nor they are as holy as you should be, and might be. You have been much occupied of late in rejoicing over accessions to our numbers, forgetting, perhaps, that each new member, seemed to bring this message from God to *you*, " Be ye holy, for I am holy, and I require you to be holy, for the sake of those who are come to have fellowship with you, in the privileges and duties of the church."

Holiness is a very comprehensive word, and expresses a state of mind and conduct that includes many things. It is the work of the Spirit in our sanctification; the fruit of faith in our Lord Jesus Christ; and the operation of the new nature, which we receive in regeneration. Holiness may be viewed in various aspects, according to the different objects to which it relates. Toward *God*, it is supreme love; delight in his moral character; submission to his will; obedience to his commands; zeal for his cause; observance of his institutes; and seeking his glory. — Toward *Christ*, it is a conformity to his example, and imbibing his spirit. — Toward *man*, it is charity, integrity, truth, mercy. — Toward *sin*, it is a hatred of all iniquity, a tender conscience easily wounded by little sins, and scrupulously avoiding them; together with a laborious, painful, self-denying, progressive mortification of all the known corruptions of our heart and a diligent seeking for such as are unknown.—Toward *self*, it is the control of our fleshly appetites; the eradication of our pride; the mortification of our selfishness.—Toward *divine things in general*, it is spirituality of mind, or the habitual current of pious thought, and devout affections flowing through the soul.—And, toward *the objects of the unseen world*, it is heavenly-mindedness, a turning away from things seen and temporal, to things unseen and eternal.

Oh, what a word is holiness! How much does it comprehend! How little is it understood, and how much less is it practised! Who can read the above description of it, and not admit that we need much, very much more of it than we possess, and that we may well make it the subject-matter of our prayers for another year. Study it as a whole, and in all its parts. How important is that view of it, which brings your conduct under the notice of men, and by whom, not only your own religion may be suspected, but all religion will be reviled, if they see any want of consistency between your actions and your profession: and how important also is that view of holiness, which considers your conduct in reference to God and Christ. To which duty, brethren, shall I most earnestly direct your attention, to a deeper spirituality, or a stricter morality? To a more elevated heavenly-mindedness, or a more uniform exhibition of the graces that shed their fragrance, and exhibit their beauty upon earth? I exhort you to seek both: I want to see the devotion of the church, incorporated with, and vitalizing and animating the morality of the house and of the shop. I want to see the spirit of prayer shedding a lustre, and diffusing the beauties of holiness over the whole character. I want to see the saint blended with and sustaining the husband, the father, the master, and the tradesman. To adopt apostolic and inspired language, I covet to see you exemplary in "*all* holy conversation and godliness."

This, then, is what I press upon you as the object to be sought by us this year, and indeed, through every future year of our lives — *more holiness*. And for whom should we seek it? For the PASTOR: that his mind may be more filled with holy light, his heart with holy love, and his life with holy actions. Do not leave *him* out of your prayers. Much, under God, even in reference to yourselves, will depend upon *him;* upon his preaching; the tone of his piety: and the wisdom, sanctity, and blamelessness of his conduct. Appointed to be an example to the flock, as well as its teacher and ruler, it is for your own advantage that you should seek for him an abundant supply of the Spirit of Christ Jesus. If apostles asked the prayers of the righteous, with how much greater propriety and correctness may *we* say — "Brethren, pray for us."

Pray for the DEACONS that they may be all men

of eminent and consistent piety; men to whom the church may look up with esteem and confidence, on account of the measure of their holy gifts, and heavenly graces; men who shall feel their responsibility in being raised to office in Christ's kingdom, and who shall give themselves, not only to the temporal, but also to the spiritual interests of the church, and be always ready, in conjunction with the pastor, to lay themselves out for promoting the growth of piety among the members.

Pray for THE WHOLE CHURCH, in its collective capacity, and in all its wide extent, and variety of circumstances, sex, and station; that it may be full of the Holy Spirit, replenished with his divine benediction, as a Spirit of holiness, and made to abound in all the fruits of righteousness, which are by Jesus Christ unto the glory of God.

Let each individual consider HIMSELF as the representative of the whole church; and as the piety of the whole body is made up of the piety of the separate members, it is his duty to begin the increase with himself. Let each seriously consider into how much higher degrees of holiness he would have the church advance, and let him immediately seek grace to advance into that state himself. Let *each* grow in grace, then *all* will grow in grace. Let each seek a revival of religion in his own soul, then the whole church will be revived. Let each, therefore, say, "I solemnly purpose and resolve, as God shall assist me, to be more holy this year than ever. I will seek to increase with all the increase of God, and to be filled with all his fulness. *My* aim and directory shall be more holiness."

But, perhaps, you would wish me to specify some points to which, above others, I would have you direct your attention, in order to an increase of holiness. Holiness consists of two general branches. The mortification of sin, and the vivification of Christian graces.

As to mortification of sin, carry on this year a more determined crucifixion of all heart-sins, all evil thoughts, and evil feelings. "Crucify the flesh, with the affections and lusts thereof." "Blessed are the pure in heart," said Christ, "for they shall see God." A real Christian should "keep the *heart* with all diligence," a duty too much neglected. We are too apt to be satisfied if the life be free from visible sins, forgetting that God seeth and searcheth the heart. Direct your attention more fixedly, and your aim more constantly, to the destruction of *besetting sins.* "Lay aside every weight," said the apostle, "and the sin that doth most easily beset you." You know what they are, whether lusts of the flesh, or lusts of the mind; whether bad tempers toward man, or sinful dispositions toward God; whether violations of piety, or of social propriety. Let this year, then, be distinguished by a great mortification of besetting sins. May we all go afresh to this work in the exercise of faith and prayer.

What a year will it be, if all of us should come to the close of it, in a state of blessed freedom from sins that had distressed us, disgraced us, and hindered us in our progress heavenward, more than anything else. No sins require such severe mortification, such incessant labor, such earnest prayer, such strong faith for their destruction as these: but all this is necessary, for if they be not destroyed, they will probably destroy us.

Connected with this, must also be *the cultivation of a tender conscience:* a conscience tender as the apple of the eye; and that shrinks from little, as well as from greater injuries. The Christian's soul is sorely injured, the credit of religion is greatly lessened, and the minds of sinners much hardened, by the little sins of professors.

But there must also be the vivification of our graces. I propose two things, GREATER SPIRITUALITY OF MIND, *i. e.*, a greater delight to think, to talk, to meditate, on spiritual subjects: a keener relish for what is divine; a more ardent and habitual delight in God; a more intense apprehension of the love of Christ; a hungering and thirsting after righteousness; a pleasure in prayer, reading the Scriptures, and attending the means of grace. And with this a HEAVENLY-MINDEDNESS, by which I mean, a sense of our pilgrimage-state on earth: a proneness to think of heaven, to long and prepare for it. In short, I intend the disposition expressed in such passages as these, "Set your affections on things above, not on things on the earth." — "Looking for that blessed hope, the glorious appearance of our great God and Savior, Jesus Christ." — "I have a desire to depart, and be with Christ." — "For we are willing rather to be absent from the body, and to be present with the Lord." This is what I am anxious to see, a *religion of the affections;* a spiritual and heavenly religion; a religion that makes you spiritual amid worldly things, and heavenly amid earthly ones.

Such are the things I propose to you, as the object of pursuit this year.

Do you not *need* them? are you holy enough, spiritual enough, heavenly enough? Can you so far impose upon yourselves, any of you, as to imagine you may be satisfied with your present attainments? God preserve you from the Laodicean mistake, of supposing you have "need of nothing."

Would you not be more *happy*, if you were more holy? Would you not thus have clearer evidence of your personal interest in the blessing of salvation, and be less troubled with doubts and fears; and at the same time experience a more blessed degree of spiritual liberty? Would you not bear your cares and troubles with greater ease and comfort?

Would you not be *more useful* by your example, your influence, your prayers, if you were more holy? And surely you cannot be indifferent to usefulness.

Would you not be thus *meetening for heaven,* and more rapidly training up for glory? Grace is glory begun, glory is grace completed; and according to your degrees of grace on earth, will be your degrees of glory in heaven.

Is not this *the design of all God's dispensations of grace and providence toward you.* For what were you chosen in Christ Jesus before the foundation of the world? To be holy. Ephes. i. 4; v. What was Christ's purpose in dying for you upon the cross? That you might be holy. Ephes. v. 26, 27. Titus ii. 11–13. For what is the Spirit poured out from on high? To make you holy. Gal. v. 16–26. Ephes. v. 22–32. John iii. 4–8. What is the nature of our calling? A holy one; "for we are called to holiness." 1 Thess. iv. 7. What is the design of the Bible? To make us holy. John xvii. 17. Why are we afflicted? "To be made partakers of his holiness. Heb. xii 10–14. What is heaven? The perfection of holiness. Ephes. v. 27. 1 John iii. 2. Rev. xxi 27; xxii. 11. See, dear brethren, how everything concurs in your being made holy.

Let me then entreat you, as your friend, your pastor, the watchman of your souls, and overseer of your spiritual interests, to strive after holiness.

Take up the subject in real earnest. Enter into the idea, and let it take full possession of your souls, *that you must be a more holy people.* Oh, if this year should be devoted to such an object, what, what, might we not expect!

In order to this,

Let it be a matter of constant, earnest, believing *prayer* in your closets, at your family altars, and in your social meetings; for it is "the Spirit of Holiness" from heaven that must make you holy. Depend upon *him*, and express your dependance by believing prayer.

Expect it: look out for it: believe that your prayers will be heard. James i. 6.

Diligently use the means of grace; not only on sabbath-days, but on week-days. Take pains to attain this state of mind. Give yourselves to it as something of importance you must attain to.

Bend everything to it; seek that your mercies may be sanctified, and your afflictions sanctified. Go to hear sermons in order to be more holy. Go to prayer-meetings to be made holy. Go to the Lord's Supper to be made holy. Read the Bible to be made holy.

Keep up *a spirit of faith* in Christ Jesus. All fulness is in him; and all supplies must be had from and through him.

Such are my wishes, my prayers, and my pursuits, concerning you. By God's grace I mean to take more pains with you, and to be more in earnest for you than ever. But this will be of no avail, unless you take pains for and with yourselves. You can no more grow in holiness, by merely wishing for it, than a child can increase in stature and strength, by desiring it, while, at the same time, he neglects all the means of growth.

Do not abuse the doctrine of the Spirit's influence, to live in indolence. The promised aid of the Spirit is to stimulate, and not to paralyze your energies. "Work out your salvation with fear and trembling, for it is God that worketh in you, to will and to do according to his good pleasure." In this instructive passage, *we* are encouraged to work, because God works.

Do not reconcile yourselves to imperfection, by the idea that there is no perfection in this world, "Having these promises, dearly beloved," says the Apostle, "let us purify ourselves from all filthiness of flesh and spirit, perfecting holiness in the fear of God." 2 Cor. vii. 1. It is obviously our duty to aim at perfection, though we shall never attain it in this world.

You are already aware that I have suggested one or two new measures for promoting your increased holiness. I have recommended the purchase and daily perusal by every one of the members of the church, of that eminently simple and spiritual little manual of piety, "BOGATZKY's GOLDEN TREASURY;" and I trust that each of you will possess the book, and as each day comes round, will read the portion allotted to it; and make it the subject of devout meditation, during the intermissions of domestic care, and secular business. It will produce a sweet and blessed fellowship of sentiment and feeling, between the members of the church, necessarily separated from each other.

I pray to God, and entreat your prayers, that I

may be assisted to write these addresses in a plain and scriptural manner: and that you may read them much to your edification. I recommend the frequent perusal of them, and that they be read the first time on the sacrament sabbath, alone in your closet of private prayer; with great solemnity, and with earnest desire to profit by them. I recommend also the perusal of the Scriptures during the month, which I shall mention; as well as the reading, at the time of the perusal of the tract, the texts referred to, but for the sake of brevity not quoted. The chapters suited to this address are, Matthew v. vi. vii. Romans vi. vii. viii. xii. Galations v. vi. Ephesians iv. v. vi. James ii. iii. 1 Peter i. ii. 2 Peter i. iii. 1 John i. ii. iii. v.

May God render this plan a means of your spiritual edification and growth in holiness. Commending you to God and the word of his grace.

No. II.

SPIRITUALITY OF MIND.

My Dear Friends: The subject of this address is "Spirituality of Mind:" a most blessed condition of the soul, much spoken of in conversation and in sermons; often discussed in books; frequently prayed for; yet little understood, and too rarely, at least in any high degree, possessed. It is a branch of holiness, but refers rather to the state of the mind, as the expression imports, than to the conduct. "*To be spiritually-minded*," says the apostle, "*is life and peace.*" Rom. viii. 7. Or, as the words may be rendered, "*the minding of the Spirit*," *i. e.*, the things of the Spirit, "is life and peace." In the preceding verse it is said, "they that are after the Spirit do mind the things of the Spirit." The word rendered "*they mind*," expresses primarily the exercise of the intellect, they *attend to*, they *employ their thoughts;* but secondarily, and by implication, the exercise of the affections. Hence, in Col. iii. 2, it is thus rendered: "Set your *affections* on things above." Spirituality of mind, then, means *the habitual and pious employment of the thoughts and affections on divine subjects.* It is something more than morality of conduct, however pure and exemplary;

more than attendance on the means of grace, however punctual; more than liberality, however diffusive; more than zeal, however active: it means, in addition to all this, *an habitual devotional state of mind.*

It is the same state of mind toward God and Christ, and divine things in general, as an affectionate husband and father has toward his wife and children, who, not only upon the whole, truly regards them, and avoids whatever is grossly inconsistent with such a profession, but whose heart, when he is absent from them, instinctively, spontaneously, and habitually, turns toward them; who needs no prompter to remind him of them; whose thoughts are confined to no time or place, and as often as they occur, and that is perpetually, kindle his affections, and make him love to talk of them, and long to be with them. Here is more than decorous conduct, here is a *minding* of them. Something like this is spirituality of mind, only the object is divine, and not human. It is such a *minding* of spiritual things as arises from interest and delight in them; such a proneness to meditate upon them as is produced by a strong attachment to them. The true indication of this state of mind, then, is to be found in the prevailing character and complexion of the *thoughts.* "As a man thinketh in his heart," says the Proverb, "so is he." Thoughts are the springs of feeling, the elements of action, and of character. The object of our thoughts in this state of mind is not merely future glory, for that we characterize heavenly-mindedness; it is not a mere looking up into heaven, a longing and craving, amid the sorrows of life, after immortality and eternal repose, but a devout and habitual reflection on the whole range of divine truth; the glorious character of God; the person and offices of Christ; the wise and gracious care of a superintending Providence; the covenant of grace; the exceeding great and precious promises of the divine word; the millenial state of the world; and the second coming of Christ, with all the other varieties of spiritual subjects.

Now if there be a spiritual mind, our thoughts of these subjects will be *voluntary* and *spontaneous;* they will rise up in the soul, not only when it is appealed to by sermons, books, and events, which in some sense compel it to think, but in the absence of the minister; when at a distance from the sanctuary; and when neither volume nor dispensation of providence speaks to us. In retirement, in solitude, on journey's, in the sleepless hours of night, and during the intervals of business, we shall turn to some topic of religion, to the glory of God, the work of Christ, or the privileges of believers, and find our comfort and joy in such meditations. We shall muse till the fire burns within us. We shall court such seasons of holy thoughtfulness, and strive to lengthen them when they occur.

Such thoughts will be *frequent* and *habitual*.

They will occur not only at long intervals, nor be looked upon, when they do, as strangers entering into the mind, surprising it by their novelty, and almost alarming it, as the vision of an angel did the Jews, under supposition that they are the harbinger of death; but they are the stated residents of the mind, necessarily going abroad for various purposes, but still returning home, as soon as that business is done, to dwell there. They are the daily, almost hourly occupants of the soul.

These thoughts are as *agreeable* to the mind as they are habitual. The Christian loves to think on divine things; they suit his taste, are congenial with his desires, and are productive of his happiness. They are as welcome as beloved friends, who are received with joy, entertained with pleasure, and parted from with reluctance.

Pious thoughts are readily *suggested by the occurrences of life* to the spiritually-minded Christian. His comforts lead him to think of the goodness of God; his afflictions of their divine source. In public judgments his mind goes up to the Supreme Governor; in national mercies to the Author of fruitful seasons and public tranquillity. Where others talk of nature, he thinks of God; and where they speak of fortune, he dwells on Providence. Recollecting the beautiful imagery of Scripture, which has associated the offices, and work, and benefits of Christ, with all the objects of nature; he sees the glories of the Savior figuratively set forth before him in the splendor of the sun, the brilliancy of the morning-star, the clustered vine, the waving corn, the tender shepherd, and the affectionate bridegroom. Without allowing his spirituality to degenerate into an allegorizing, rhapsodical, or mystic piety, he loves to follow in the track of the sacred writers, and read his Savior's name in those objects on which they have imprinted it. And I may remark that among all the objects to which the thoughts and affections of the spiritually-minded are directed, the person and work of our Lord Jesus Christ stand pre-eminent. They do not stop in the contemplation of God, and Providence, and heaven but contemplate all in Christ, and Christ in all. His divinity, atonement, and intercession; his perfect righteousness for justification, and his spotless example as the rule of their sanctification; his offices of prophet, priest, and king, are all themes which have irresistible attractions for their thoughts. Nothing more decidedly indicates spirituality, than this habitual tendency of the thoughts to Christ. It is not heaven, merely, nor chiefly, I again repeat, that this disposition leads the believer to dwell upon, but Christ; for what is heaven but the presence of Christ? Provided he could see the glory, and feel the grace of the Savior, it is all one to the man of strong faith, the advanced Christian, whether he is in heaven or upon earth, or at any rate, his desire to depart is founded on the hope and desire of a more perfect fusion and enjoyment of Christ. The degree to which our thoughts and feelings are drawn to the Redeemer, is the precise amount we possess of true spirituality of mind. There may be, and doubtless is, much serious reflection of a certain kind, compelled by sorrow, or produced by a sentimental turn of mind, on various generalities of religion, and especially upon Providence and heaven, even where there is no evangelical piety. But to them that believe Christ is precious. He is the specific object and centre of their devotional reflections.

The thoughts of the truly spiritually-minded always *kindle religious affections* and *lead to corresponding actions*. Spirituality of mind is not mere silent contemplation, inactive sentimentality, passionless quietism; no, it is habitual and delightful *thinking*, producing habitual and delightful *feeling*, and ending in habitual *holy actions*. "It is of little consequence what are our musings, and meditations, and heart-stirring feelings, and elevated thoughts, unless there is connected with all these excitements, what is the only legitimate proof of their genuineness and sincerity, conformity to the will of God, and actual meetness for heaven, in our temper, disposition, and character." It is a spurious spirituality, and one of the artifices by which Satan deceives and destroys unwary souls, to indulge in pious thoughts, and luxuriate in devotional feeling, while the temper is unsubdued, the corruptions of the heart unmortified, and the actions of the life are in little conformity with the word of God.

Such is spirituality of mind; not a mere religious talkativeness, which confines itself to a set of current phrases, and which is ever forward to obtrude them upon all persons and on all occasions; not affected grimace, and fawning pious obsequiousness; nothing of the sort. True it is, that the person enjoying this holy state of soul, will be ever willing, yea, ready to converse with others, like minded, on the subjects nearest and dearest to their hearts, and it is one of the marks of their character to solicit as companions, and to associate habitually with those who are qualified by their experience and prepared by their disposition, to engage in such discourse as befits the redeemed of the Lord, and the travellers to immortality. Shunning the worldly-minded, the political, and the controversial, they will unite with those who fear the Lord, and speak often to one another on the common salvation; but they will not indulge in what may be denominated mere cant, words which proceed from no conviction or emotion, and which end in no action.

This, my dear flock, is the state of mind which I am anxious to promote in you, and to set you an example of it in myself. It is not enough that we be outwardly correct in our conduct, and that we maintain all the forms of godliness; but we must seek to maintain the vitality of all this in the state of our minds and hearts. Religion is a living principle in the soul; yea, a divine life, a holy taste, whose seat and centre is in the mind. Conduct is but the body of character, and however symmetrical it may be, and however fair to look upon, it is pious thoughts and feeling that give it intellect and heart, and constitute its soul, without which there is but the picture or the statue, but not the living Christian. It is the object of the present address to promote the exercise of such thoughts and such affections, as may be supposed to dwell in a soul renewed by the Spirit of God, sanctified by the truth, that loves God supremely, and is under the constraining influence of the love of Christ; and is hoping, waiting, and preparing for eternal glory. And do, my dear friends, reflect what spontaneous, numerous, delightful, and practical thoughts such a state of soul might be supposed to call forth. Can a soul be redeemed, regenerated, and going to glory everlasting, and not think much, and feel much, and talk much about it? Can such prospects be before us, such hopes in us, such brightness beaming upon us, and yet there be no habitual *minding* of *such* matters?

It may be useful to mention some proofs of a want of spirituality, that those who are destitute of it, may take warning, and seek to have the defect supplied. When there is no disposition or tendency to indulge in ho y thoughts, but the whole character and complexion of the mind are worldly — when there is a disinclination to attend the week-day services of religion — when the do mestic and private duties of devotion are little better than heartless forms — when the taste in regard to sermons is rather for talent and elegance than for sound evangelical truth — when the society of worldly and political men is preferred to the company of the godly, or when the least spiritual of the latter are more sought after, and their discourse is more relished than that of the eminently pious — when cheerfulness degenerates into levity, and there is no pleasure in religious conversation — when there is a disposition to decry as hypocrisy and cant all spiritual taste and conversation — in all these cases there is a sad indication of a want of the state of mind, which it is the object of this address to promote.

But I will now enumerate some of *the principal means by which spirituality of mind may be promoted.* It will not grow in the soul without culture; nor come to us at the careless beckoning of indolent wishing. This kind goeth not forth but by fasting and prayer.

We must *set our hearts upon it*, or we shall never have it, and consider it both as a rich privilege to be enjoyed, and an incumbent duty to be performed.

The most direct and certain means of obtaining it are, *a clear scriptural knowledge af divine truth*, and *a strong faith in its glorious and eternal realities.* We cannot expect spiritual thoughts and affections from truths which are but imperfectly understood, or doubtfully and feebly believed.

How fervently should we *pray for it*, how ardently should we long for it, how laboriously should we seek for it, how confidently expect it, and how perseveringly and patiently wait for it. The prayer of faith and fervor must go up to the treasury of heaven, and fetch the blessing from the inexhaustible stores of divine grace. It is in the closet of private devotion where we commune with our Father in secret, that this pious state of mind must be cultivated, and much time for prayer must be redeemed from the world to obtain it. If you will not always pray and not faint; if you will not give yourselves to prayer, if you will not watch unto prayer, you cannot attain to this delightful state of soul. It is the Spirit's richest donation, which he bestows only on the soul that lays hold on his strength, and seems to say, "I will not let thee go except thou bless me."

Then there must be much devout *reading of the Holy Scriptures*. It is not enough not to neglect the Bible for the newspaper, but it must not be displaced by pious uninspired books. The best books of men can be no substitute for the book of God. No fuel is so meet to feed the flame of devotion as the promises, precepts, and consolations of the word of God: a single text has sometimes kept it burning with intense brightness for hours, and supplied a source of holy thoughts for a whole sleepless night or anxious day.

Meditation is of great power to promote this devout frame. We must pause and think upon the word of God till its truths expand before us and we feel its power upon the heart. Some of its minuter beauties, hidden from the hasty and superficial reader, come out to the admiring mind of him who looks attentively for them. It would be well to *fix upon a passage of Scripture in the morning*, and make it the subject of meditation, to fill up the intervals of business during the day, and be a topic always at hand for the mind to turn to in moments of leisure, and which should thus gather up for a holy purpose, these fragments of time which would otherwise be wasted on trifles, or spent on something worse. BOGATZKY will help you here.

When Christians meet they should endeavor to introduce some topic of conversation of a holy nature, and a common interest, and not allow the time to be lost, or their influence upon each other be at best negative. Large parties are unfriendly to this, as it is impossible or difficult to maintain a conversation in such circumstances, where all shall take a part. The parties even of Christians are not always favorable to their Christianity. Where the time is spent in music, singing, or mere gossip, it is but little calculated to promote spirituality of mind.

Self-examination and self-inspection must be added. We should look into our minds, and keep a constant eye upon the state of our soul, as to the thoughts and feelings that habitually dwell there, or even come as visiters. Evil thoughts keep out good ones; and even worldly ones may so crowd the mind as to leave no room for better reflections. It would be well sometimes at the close of the day, when alone in our closet, to ask the question, "What have I been thinking about to-day? How many thoughts have I given to Christ, and heaven?"

It should be a matter of special importance with us, not only to be regular and diligent in attending upon the ordinances of religion, but to be *spiritual in the use of them.* Nothing tends more to flatten devotional feeling, than an undevout attendance on religious exercises.

Ejaculatory prayer maintained throughout the day has a blessed effect. It would keep the heart in a sweet and holy temper all the day long, and have an excellent influence on all our ordinary actions and common duties. This were to "walk with God" indeed, to hold continually by our Father's hand; whereas, without this, our praying morning and evening looks but as a formal visit not delighting in that constant converse, which is yet our happiness and honor, and makes all conditions to be pleasant, all places to be sacred, and all occupations profitable. "This would refresh us in the hardest labor, as they that carry away the spices from Arabia, are refreshed by the scent of them in their journey, and some observe that it keeps their strength, and prevents them from fainting."

And as we should be *less worldly in our spiritual matters*, so we should be *more spiritual in our worldly ones.* "Not only labor," says pious LEIGHTON, "to keep thy mind spiritual in itself, but by it put a spiritual stamp even upon thy temporal employments; and so thou shalt live to God, not only without prejudice of thy calling, but even in it, and shalt converse with him in thy shop, or in the field, or in thy journey, doing all in obedience to him, and offering all, and thyself withal, as a sacrifice to him; thou still with him, and he still with thee, in all. This is to live to the will of God indeed, to follow his direction, and intend his glory in all. Thus the wife in the very oversight of her house, and the husband in his affairs abroad, may be living to God, raising their low employments to a high quality this way;" Lord, even this mean work I do for thee, complying with thy will, who has put me in this station, and given me this task. "Thy will be done." Lord, I offer up even this work to thee. Accept of me, and of my desire to obey thee in all. And as in their work, so in their refreshments and rest, Christians do all for him. "Whether ye eat or drink," says the apostle, 1 Cor. x. 31, "or whatsoever ye do, do all for the glory of God;" doing all for this reason, because it is his will, and for this end, that he may have glory; bending the use of all our strength and all his mercies that way; setting this mark on all our designs and way. This for the glory of my God, and this farther for his glory, and so from one thing to another throughout our whole life. This is the art of keeping the heart spiritual in all affairs, yea, spiritualizing the affairs themselves in their use, that in themselves are earthly. This is the elixir that turns lower metal into gold, the mean actions of this life, in a Christian's hands, into obedience and holy offerings unto God.

How many MOTIVES urge you to the cultivation of this divine temper. Some degree of it is essentially necessary to the very existence of personal religion. "To be carnally-minded is *death*, but to be spiritually-minded is life and peace." The soul that has no degree of this holy heavenly temper, is dead in trespasses and sins. *No* tendency to pious thoughts and affections, is the characteristic of a soul, in which no spark of the divine life is yet kindled. But I am not now urging the necessity of regeneration, but of higher degrees of sanctification, and a larger measure of spirituality, as an essential part of it.

Think of the *happiness* accompanying a large share of spirituality. It is life and peace; a living peace; a peaceful life. It is *life;* just as much as we have of this and no more, we have of the life of God, of heaven, of holiness in our souls. All life in sentient beings is delightful in proportion to its vigor and healthfulness; the sensations of animal life are agreeable; the exercises of intellectual life still more so; but the actings and aspirations of spiritual life, are the sublimest felicity the human soul can know: this is the life of spirits made perfect: of the blessed angels; of our Lord Jesus Christ; and of the great God himself, who is pure spirit. In the exercises of this life, we therefore have fellowship with the Father, and with his Son Jesus Christ. This is the life whose spring is hid with Christ in God. Let us rise higher, my dear friends, into this lofty and holy existence. As rational creatures it is a dignified employment to use our noble faculties in the contemplation of the works of creation, but as spiritual ones it is still more dignified, to use them in contemplating and enjoying the things that are above, where Christ sitteth on the right hand of God. This is indeed peace, a word that signifies not only tranquillity and repose of mind, but all the kinds and parts of substantial happiness. There is no real felicity out of the region of divine realities, and it is spirituality that brings us within this hallowed circle, and enables us to drink the crystal waters of these blessed springs.

If you would enjoy religion, then, or at any rate, if you would have a rich and powerful enjoyment of it, you must attain to high degrees of this devout temper. Think of the felicity which a current of holy thoughts flowing through the soul, and directing its course ever toward God, and Christ, and heaven, must bring with it. How richly must such a stream be impregnated with all the elements of a paradisaic life. How would such a state of mind lighten your cares, alleviate your sorrows, sweeten your comforts, sanctify your trials, elevate your devotions, and anticipate heaven. How many otherwise cheerless scenes would it enliven, and how many gloomy seasons would it irradiate! What a source of perennial delight would it open, where all beside is a desert of the soul. Blessed state, day and night to be conversant with holy, heavenly, peaceful thoughts.

Perhaps some of you have not *lost* this spirituality, because you have never attained to any high degrees of it. "What is the source of your most poignant regrets — what most powerfully awakens the bitter feelings of self-reproach — renders the means of grace unproductive of joy, and exposes you to the most dangerous excursions of your spiritual foes? Is it not when you are 'minding the things of the flesh,' and not 'minding the things of the Spirit?' It is the want of spirituality that beclouds your prospects, causes darkness, and doubt, and fear, to surround your path — obscures the evidences of your interest in the divine favor — gives power to your invisible enemies, and leads either to the experience of painful and morbid dejection, or the more dangerous feeling of unholy presumption."*

Think of what importance spirituality of mind is *to give life, and beauty, and attractive force to your example.* It is this which, when added to outward consistency of conduct, presents religion to the world as it really is, a divine and heavenly thing

" On Spirituality of Mind," by Dr. FLETCHER. An admirable little pocket-companion which I most earnestly recommend to my friends.

upon earth: for though its seat is in the soul, yet by the intensity and brightness of an inward flame, it sends out a lustre over the whole character, and exhibits the beauties of holiness in a state of illumination. Or, to change the metaphor, though the principle of life be within, it presents the outer man of piety as a vital reality, and not a dead form.

You may be *useful* I admit, without much, or even without any spirituality; for God can glorify himself by the instrumentality of unconverted men; but how much *more* useful may you be if all the offerings of your liberality are salted with this grace, and the flame of your zeal be fed with the oil of this personal piety. What a prevalence will it give to your prayers, what an impulse to your liberality, and what a constancy as well as steadfastness to your energies and efforts.

And is it not thus you are to become meet to be partakers of the inheritance of the saints in light? Yea, is it not the beginning of heaven upon earth? What is heaven, but the absence of all that is carnal, and the presence and perfection of all that is spiritual? It is by the habitual recurrence of holy thoughts that the lineaments of a heavenly character are impressed upon the soul, and by the ardor of holy affections, that they acquire an unfading beauty and an enduring form.

No. III.

HEAVENLY-MINDEDNESS.

My Dear Friends: The subject of this address is *heavenly-mindedness*. It may seem, perhaps, that there is considerable sameness in these first three letters of the series which it is my intention to lay before you. That they are alike and related, I admit, but not that they are identical; and, indeed, they are selected on account of their relation to each other, and with the hope of mutually aiding to deepen, by the repetition and concentration of one train of thought, the impression which each by itself, and the three together, are intended to produce.

Heavenly-mindedness is an expression that explains itself, it is the *minding* of heaven; or the exercise of tho thoughts and affections upon those invisible but eternal realities, which are declared by the Scriptures to await the Christian beyond the grave. Spirituality is one branch of holiness; and heavenly-mindedness is spirituality, exercised in reference to one specific object — the celestial state.

Alas! how little of this is there to be found even among professing Christians: —

> "How low their hopes of heaven above,
> How few affections there."

The description given by the apostle of the predominant taste and pursuits of the men of the world — "They mind earthly things" — too well suits a large proportion of those who in profession have come out from the world, and are a people separate unto God. How engrossed are they, not only in the business, but in the cares, the love, and the enjoyment of earth. Who would imagine, to see their conduct, to hear their conversation, to observe their spirit, so undevout, and so worldly, that these were the men, who have heaven in their eye, their heart, their hope? Even to them, we should be inclined to think, that the Paradise of God is nothing more than a name, a sublime fiction, a sacred vision, which, with all its splendor, has scarcely power enough to engage their thoughts and fix their regards. How little effect has it to elevate them above a predominant earthly-mindedness, to comfort them in trouble, to minister to their happiness, or to mortify their corruptions. Can it be that *they* are seeking for, and going to glory, honor, and immortality, who think so little about it, and derive so small a portion of their enjoyment from the expectation of it?

What is heaven? The Bible and the Bible only, can answer this question: and even this, though a revelation from God, but partially discloses the infinite and eternal reality. There is enough to excite, sustain, and animate hope, but far too little to gratify curiosity. Substantials are revealed, circumstantials are withheld. You cannot be ignorant that heaven is represented in the Bible, rather as *a state of mind*, than as a *place;* and that where objects of sense and locality are spoken of, they are to be understood, for the most part, in a figurative, and not in a literal meaning. The description of the celestial world, as we find it in the Word of God, has always appeared to me one of the most striking and convincing of the internal evidences of Christianity. The Elysium of the Greeks and Romans; the Paradise of Mahomet, and the various fantastic ideas of the world beyond the grave, entertained by modern pagans, are all of the earth, earthly; nothing more or better than earthly and sensual gratifications rendered immortal. How different the heaven of the New Testament; how pure, how spiritual, how unearthly, how divine! How strictly in harmony with the sublime and holy character of God! How befitting a creature, intelligent and holy! How completely different from everything which the unholy, sensual, and earthly mind of man would ever have devised! How far remote from the track of all his thoughts!

Heaven is usually called *eternal life, i. e., eternal happy existence:* everlasting existence, with all that can render existence a blessing. But what are the elements of its felicity? As regards our own condition, they consist of a soul, possessed of perfect knowledge, perfect holiness, perfect liberty, perfect love, united with a body raised from the grave, incorruptible, immortal, and spiritual. As regards our relations to other beings, heavenly bliss means our dwelling in the immediate presence of Christ; the perfect vision, service, likeness, and enjoyment of God: the society and converse of angels, and the spirits of just men made perfect. Connected with this, is the absence of everything that annoys, disturbs, or distresses us in this life. Such is the scripture-representation of heaven, as will be seen by consulting the following scriptures. Psalm xvi. 11; xvii. 15. John iii. 14, 15, 36; xvii. 24. Rom. ii. 7; viii. 18. 1 Cor. xv. 2 Cor. iv. 17. Philip i. 21; iii. 21. Heb. iv. 9; xii. 22–24. 1 John iii. 2. Rev. vii. 9–17; xxi., xxii.

"My chief conception of heaven," said ROBERT HALL to WILBERFORCE, "*is rest.*"—"Mine," replied WILBERFORCE, "is LOVE; love to God, and love to every bright and holy inhabitant of that glorious place." HALL was an almost constant sufferer from acute bodily pain; WILBERFORCE enjoyed life, and was all amiability and sunshine; so that it is easy to account says Mr. GURNEY, "for their respective conceptions of this subject. What a mercy that both these conceptions are true." Yes, both *are* true; and the union of rest and love, perhaps, conveys, within a small compass, the most correct idea of the heavenly state.

Following the order of the representation given in the address on Spirituality of Mind, I observe that *heavenly*-mindedness means the *spontaneous frequent*, *delightful*, *practical* bent of our reflecions toward eternal life. A heavenly-minded man is one who, as a convinced, condemned sinner, having obtained a title to eternal life, through faith in the blood and righteousness of Christ, and a meetness for it, in the regenerating work of the Holy Spirit, considers himself as a pilgrim and stranger upon earth: regards heaven as his native country, and as instinctively turns his thoughts to it, as he who in a distant part of the world, feels his mind and heart attracted to his home. Scarcely a day passes during which no thought of his mind, no glance of the eye of faith, turns to the glory to be revealed. In his solitary musings in the house, or by the way, the object is present to his mind to occupy his thoughts, to refresh and delight his spirit: and when he is with others like-minded with himself, it is his delight to converse upon the country to which they are travelling. Precious to him are those parts of revelation which speak of the life to come, and exhibit to him, amid the darkness of his way, the distant lights of his father's house. Sermons that represent the holiness and happiness of heaven are delightful to his heart; books that describe it are congenial with his taste; and the songs of Zion, which sounds like the echo of its divine harmonies, excite all his hallowed sensibilities, and elevate his spirit to catch some of the falling rays of the excellent glory. The beautiful symbols of heavenly bliss, the city too bright with inherent splendor to need the sun; the walls of jasper, the gates of pearl, and streets of pure gold, like unto clear glass; the crown of life; the harp of gold; the palm of victory; the white robe; the song of salvation sounding from the countless multitude of the redeemed; all by turns seize and fix his imagination; while his enlightened judgment and his holy heart, letting go these brilliant images, repose upon the realities they are intended to portray, the presence of God, the vision of the Lamb, the sinless purity, the eternal rest, the communion of the blessed, the fellowship of angels.

The heavenly-minded man not only employs his *thoughts*, but sets his *affections* on things above. His hope and his heart are there. He does not wish it, it would not be proper that he should, instantly to dissolve his ties with earth, and leaving his family and connexions fly next moment home: he is willing to wait as long as it is his heavenly Father's will to detain him upon earth, but he is willing to quit all and go to God, whenever it is judged proper by him to decide the matter, that he should go up to the mount and die. His hopes of heaven do much to destroy his love of life, and fear of death. If nature shrinks, as it sometimes will, at the approach of dissolution, he looks beyond the gloomy passage, and anticipates by a lively hope, the moment when "lifting his last step from the wave, having passed the stream of death, he shall linger and look wondrously back upon its dark waters, then gilded with the light of immortality, and rippling peacefully on the eternal shore."

It is not in suffering only that he feels a longing after immortality, for it is no indication of heavenly-mindedness to wish to depart in order to get rid of trouble. Impatience to die is often felt by those who have ceased to feel any attractions in life, and the grave is coveted as a shelter from the storms of earth. There is nothing holy in such wishes; nothing heavenly in such impatience; it is only nature groaning after rest, and not grace longing for its perfection. Perhaps the most holy frame is to have no will or wish about the matter, but a readiness to live or die as God shall appoint. If, however, a preference may be cherished, and the soul rises into a longing to depart, the only ground on which it can with propriety be indulged is, an earnest desire to get rid of sin, to be near and like Christ, to serve God more perfectly, and to glorify him more entirely: and such desires after immortality, when no tie binds us to earth, are legitimate and holy. Happy moments there sometimes are, alas! how rare, in the experience of the spiritual Christian, when such are his views of the desirableness of heaven, that he feels as if he should be glad to break down the prison-walls of his spirit, and let her go forth into the liberty of her eternal felicity. The celebrated John Howe once had such a view of heaven, and such a desire to depart, that he said to his wife: "Though I think I love you as well as it is fit for one creature to love another, yet if it were put to my choice, whether to die this moment, or live through this night; and living this night would secure the continuance of life for seven years longer, I would choose to die this moment." Still the glory of a Christian is to be neither weary of the world nor fond of it; to be neither afraid of death nor impatient after it; to be willing to go to heaven the next hour from the greatest comforts, or to wait for it through many lingering years, amid the greatest hardships, the most self-denying and laborious duties, and the severest and most complicated sufferings.

The heavenly-minded man goes farther than this, and *prepares* for future glory. Considering heaven not merely as an object of delightful contemplation, of devout imagination, or of holy revery — a sublime and splendid picture for a visionary piety to gaze upon — but as a state of moral being, action, and service, for which a meetness is required — he diligently cultivates those dispositions which the Word of God assures him belong to, and are to be exercised in the celestial state. He has a post to fill, a situation to occupy, a service to perform in heaven, and for which he knows the necessary qualifications must be acquired on earth. Death is only a *physical* change, and as far as we can understand, produces no *moral* effect. Grace is the preparation for glory, and he who has most grace, is most meetened for glory. The man who is going to occupy a place in the palace, endeavors to acquire courtly manners, and to provide himself with a court dress. So the eminently-spiritual Christian considers himself as going in to dwell in the palace of the King of kings, and his great business upon earth is to prepare himself with the qualifications and dress of the celestial court. And as he clearly perceives that the prevailing dispositions of heaven are purity and love, he labors to grow in holiness and charity. If asked, in any situation or circumstance, or at any period, what are you engaged in or employed about? his answer is, "I am dressing for heaven; making myself ready to go in and dwell with Christ. Having a post to fill in the divine palace, I am preparing for it by the mortification of sin, and a growth in grace."

Such is heavenly-mindedness: but, alas! where is it to be found? I know where it ought to be found — in every professing Christian. His principles demand it, his profession requires it, his prospects justify it. "If we should give a stranger to Christianity an account of the Christian's hopes, and tell him what Christians are, and what they expect to enjoy ere long, he would sure promise himself to find so many angels dwelling in human flesh, and reckon when he came among them, he should be as amid the heavenly choir; every one full of joy and praise. He would expect to find us living on earth as the inhabitants of heaven; as so many pieces of immortal glory, lately dropped down from above, and shortly returning thither again. He would look to find everywhere in the Christian world incarnate glory, sparkling through the overshadowing veil; and wonder how this earthly sphere should be able to contain so many great souls." And oh, how astonished, surprised, and disgusted would he be to witness the earthly-mindedness, and to hear the worldly conversation of the great bulk of professing Christians, as if heaven were nothing more than a splendid painting to adorn their temples of religion, and to be looked at once a week; but not a glorious reality to be ever before their eyes, to form their character, to regulate their conduct, support them in trouble, and furnish their chief happiness!

What a source of *strong consolation* and *ineffable delight* is a heavenly mind to its possessors. This is what the apostle calls "*rejoicing in hope of the glory of God.*" Could we actually look into the celestial world, and see its felicities and honors; could we hear the very sounds of paradise, and have the songs of the redeemed continually, or at intervals, undulating on our ear; could the rays of the excellent glory, literally fall upon our path: how constantly should we go on our way rejoicing, as we reflected that each step brought us nearer to this world of light and love; and of purity and immortality! How soft would be the cares, how tolerable the sorrows, how easy the most difficult duties, so soon to be laid aside amid such rest and such happiness! This sight of heaven would irradiate the darkest scenes of earth, and prevent us from being seduced by the beauties of the fairest. Who could weep while heaven was spreading out its glories to comfort us, and opening its doors to receive us! Who could think much of that sickness which was sustained beneath the vision of an incorruptible inheritance, or of those losses which came upon them in sight of an infinite portion that never fades away! There would need no amusement or recreation to make us happy, while listening to the song of salvation: nor of any other pleasure to cheer us: this mixture of the view of heaven with the scenes of earth, would change the aspect of everything, and give truth to the expressions of the poet —

> "The men of grace have found,
> Glory begun below."

And what more than a heavenly mind, a vigorous, lively, and influential faith, is necessary to give something like a reality to this? Heaven does exist; all these glories are above us and before us, though we see them not; and it is only to believe them as they may be, and ought to be believed, and we shall rejoice in them with joy unspeakable and full of glory. Vivacious thoughts of them would, in measure, produce the same kind of happiness as seeing them. Happy should we be amid all the cares, and labors, and sorrows, and trials of earth, if in meditation, and by faith and hope, we could thus dwell on the borders of the promised land. It would be to pitch our tent on Mount Pisgah, and constantly to have the promised land spreading out in boundless and beautiful perspective before us.

Nor is it our *comfort* only that would be promoted by a heavenly mind, but our *sanctity* also. "Every man that hath this hope in him," says the apostle, "purifieth himself even as he is pure." 1 John iii. 3. Heaven, being a holy state, yea, the very perfection of holiness, does, by a natural process, render those holy who meditate upon it, believe it, hope for it, and long for it. Men's hopes always affect their conduct, and transform their characters into a likeness to the nature of the objects of their desires and expectations. How effectually guarded from temptation to concupiscence, worldly-mindedness, and malice, is he whose affections are strongly fixed upon a state of purity, spirituality, and love! Who that is drinking happiness from the crystal river that flows from the throne of God and the Lamb, can take up with the filthy puddle of worldly amusements? What mortification of sin, what conquest of besetting corruption, what eradication of evil tempers, what suppression of unholy disposition goes on, when the soul fixes the eye of faith on things unseen and eternal! Yea, what discoveries of hidden and unsuspected sins are made, when the light of heavenly glory is let into the soul! In looking so much to earth, and earthly-minded men, we become so familiarized with sin, as to lose our clear perceptions, our accurate discrimination of its evil nature, and our accurate sensibilities to its criminality and odiousness. We lose our self-abhorrence for our own sins, by the view of so much evil without and around us: and we recover our keenness of vision, and tenderness of conscience, only by lifting up our eyes to that pure and blessed region, where no sin dwells, and holiness is in perfection; and where

> One view of Jesus as he is,
> Will strike all sin for ever dead.

You will much wish to know how such a state of mind may be promoted.

You must be willing to have it. Willing! you exclaim, with somewhat of surprise, "Who is *not* willing? Who would not enjoy such a frame?" *You*, perhaps, who ask the question. Comparatively few are willing to be heavenly-minded. The great bulk even of professing Christians do not want this state of the soul; they want to enjoy earth; they are ever seeking new devices by which to be more and more gratified by things seen and temporal; they are ever seeking to invest *earth* with new charms, and to throw greater attractions over the scenes that surround them. They do not wish to have the luxuriance of their earthly affections repressed, or the exuberance of their worldly joys restrained. It is no part of their plan, or wish, or effort, or prayer, to have one single terrestrial delight limited or displaced by such as are heavenly. Very *few* are willing then, to be heavenly-minded: and if not willing, they will never attain to it.

You must be not only *willing* but *desirous* of this frame. It must appear to you a state to be coveted and longed for; and for which you would be willing to part with some of the joys of sense, and the pleasures of earth: to endure the discipline of trial, and the influence of sorrow. Your heart must be set upon it, your soul must pant after it.

It must appear to you not only desirable, but *attainable*. No such idea must be in your mind as that it is too high an elevation of piety for *you* to reach, too difficult an acquirement for *you* to make. Do not imagine that it is the devotion of the cloister and the cell, and which can be cultivated only by the recluse. Spiritual and heavenly Christians have been found, too rarely I admit, amid all the cares of a large family, and all the urgency of an extensive trade. Besides, if you cannot attain to as much of this celestial temper as some others, may you not have much more of it than you already possess. Do not even *your* circumstances allow of improvement and increase.

Use the right means for acquiring it. Believe its reality. Your faith is too weak to be influential. It is not so much a deep conviction, a full persuasion, a confident anticipation, as a mere opinion. You have the name of heaven upon your lips, but not the grand idea, the glorious reality in your mind: the infinite, the transcendent conception, does not occupy and fill the soul. You are too much a stranger to the force of that expression, " LAY HOLD *on eternal life.*"

Acquire a clear and satisfactory evidence of your personal interest in the joys and glories of immortality. "Give all diligence *to the full assurance of hope* unto the end." Unite the full assurance of hope, with the full assurance of understanding and of faith. What is our own, more interests us, though it be little, than what belongs to another, though it be far greater. The heir of a small estate has his mind and heart far more occupied about his little patrimony, than about the vast domain contiguous to it, of some wealthy peer. Realize your personal interest in heaven. If you are indeed a child of God, seek the witness of the spirit to your sonship; and if a child, then you are an heir of God, and joint heir with Christ. After reading the gracious promises, and surveying the boundless prospects of eternal glory, indulge the thoughts that these are all *yours; yours* to be admitted to the presence of God and Christ, and to dwell there for ever; *yours* to be like God and Christ in purity, love, knowledge, and immortality; *yours* to be the everlasting companion of all holy angels and blessed spirits. Call the joys of heaven your own: they will then be infinitely more attractive than they now are.

Give yourselves time for reading, meditation, and prayer. You must keep the world within due bounds as to the time it occupies. If you allow it to take and keep the occupance of the whole day, from the time you open your eyes in the morning, till you close them at night, you cannot grow in this grace. If you resist not its engrossing, absorbing power, your soul *must* suffer, your salvation be endangered, your heaven be lost. Oh, will you, with glory, honor, immortality above you, and before you, allow yourselves to be so engaged, as to have no time to think of them, or to look at them! With the splendor of heavenly and eternal glory beaming upon your path, blazing around you, will you be so taken up with the world, as to hurry by and not turn aside to see this great sight! Oh, Christians, believers, at least *professed* believers in immortality, is it thus you treat the heaven which occupied the thoughts of God from eternity, which was procured by the death of Christ upon the cross, which is the substance of revealed truth, and the end of all God's dispensations of providence and grace to man! What! no time to retire and meditate on eternal life! Will you, can you, dare you bring yourself to utter such an expression as this, "I am really so taken up with my business, that I cannot retire to meditate and pray." Then I must tell you, you have no time to be saved, though plenty of time to be lost.

Go into your closet, and with your Bible as the telescope that brings eternal glories near, meditate, meditate upon heaven. Survey its glories; go over them in detail and in succession, dwell upon the presence of God; upon being with Christ; upon perfect love, perfect purity, perfect liberty, perfect knowledge, perfect bliss. Contemplate their infinity, their immensity, their eternity. Oh, wha thoughts, what topics, what sources of delight! What sublime, elevating subjects for the child of Adam, of dust, of sin, of sorrow, of mortality, to indulge in! What a reflection upon us, that we should need to be admonished to turn our thoughts that way; that with heaven open before us, we should need to be reminded, "There is immortal glory, look at it;" and yet after all should feel that we are so pre-occupied and engaged, that we have no time to survey the wondrous scene. Dwell much upon *the nearness* of heaven. What is remote has less power over the thoughts than that which is contiguous. How near is all this glory to your soul! Nothing separates you from it, but the thin partition of flesh and blood: a moment of time, a point of space, may be all that intervenes between you and immortality. When you lie down to rest any night, you know not but you may be in heaven before the next morning. When you rise up in the morning, but that you may be in heaven before night. If you are true Christians, you are ever in the vestibule of the heavenly temple, waiting for the opening of the door, to be admitted to the holy of holies. The heirs of glory are every moment going in to be for ever with the Lord, and you will soon go with them. Heaven is ever as near to you as God is, for it is the enjoyment of his presence, and he compasseth you about on every side. At any given moment of your existence, you know not but that the next may be the commencement of your eternal career of holiness, knowledge, and happiness. Did you realize this thought, how would it tend to keep up the frame of mind I am so anxious to promote.

As heaven consists of enjoying the divine presence, and of holiness and love, together with the joy arising from them, let us seek *more intimate communion with God now,* and labor after more purity, more benevolence, more spiritual peace. This would make us think of heaven, and long for it, when we had these, its first fruits, in our soul now. We cannot go up into heaven, without heaven first comes down into us. Holiness in the soul of man is a part of heaven, and the greater heaven above will put forth an attraction to draw up to itself this lesser heaven below. Fire ascends to the sun; rivers run to the ocean; matter gravitates to its centre; so holiness in the soul aspires to heaven, to which it belongs.

And withal you must be much in private, earnest, and believing *prayer for the supply of the Spirit of Christ Jesus.* Who is sufficient for these things, but he whose sufficiency is of God the Spirit? To make the future predominate over the present; the invisible over the visible; the immaterial over the material; and heaven over earth, is an achievement of faith, to which he only is equal, who is taught and helped of God. "He that hath wrought us for this self-same thing," says the apostle, "is God, who also hath given unto us the earnest of the Spirit." 2 Cor. v. 5.

Believers in Christ Jesus; children of God heirs of immortal glory; traveller to Zion; possessors of eternal life; look not at the things which are seen and temporal, but at the things which are unseen and eternal. Think of what is before you in the world to which you are going. Let your character and your destiny be in harmony. Born *from* heaven, and bound *to* it, let your conversation be *in* heaven, "whence we look for the coming of our Lord Jesus Christ, who shall change our vile body, that it be made like unto his glorious body, according to the mighty power whereby he is able to subdue all things to himself." Phil. iii. 20, 21.

No. IV.

ASSURANCE OF HOPE.

My Dear Friends: The subject on which I address you this month is of great importance to your spiritual enjoyment, and, indeed, you cannot enter deeply into the consolations of the Spirit, without an experimental acquaintance with it; I mean, *the Assurance of Hope*. A Christian is, or might be, the happiest man upon the earth; but in order to this, he must have some satisfactory reason to conclude that he is a Christian. Religion is intended to make us happy, it is the overflowing of the felicity of the blessed God, into the soul of man; the reflection of his smiling countenance from the redeemed, regenerated spirit; and the communion of the finite mind, in the fulness of the grace and glory belonging to the infinite one; but then we must know that we *have* religion.

There are three kinds of assurance spoken of in the Word of God: 1. "The assurance of *understanding*," Col. ii. 2; which means, a clear, comprehensive, heart-establishing acquaintance with divine truth. 2. "The assurance of *faith*," Heb. x. 22; which signifies an entire persuasion of the truth of the gospel. 3. "The assurance of *Hope*," Heb. vi. 11; which imports a confidence of personal interest in Christ. It is of the latter I treat in this address. They are all three intimately related to, and grow out of each other. In proportion as we fully know and are spiritually taught the doctrines of the gospel, we shall be fully assured of their truth, and have the assurance of faith; and in exact proportion as we are fully assured of the divine person, mission, and work of Christ, we shall be fully assured of our personal interest in them, faith being based upon knowledge, and hope upon faith. The assurance of knowledge and faith has reference to the gospel in itself; the assurance of hope to the state of our heart in reference to the gospel. The assurance of faith is called for in a man's first profession of the gospel, in order to his being acknowledged as a Christian. The assurance of hope, again, is an enjoyment proposed to them that believe, and have already begun the Christian race, which they are called to follow after, and to give all diligence to obtain.

It does not appear to be necessary to this state of mind, that we should have such a persuasion as utterly and continually excludes every shade or doubt; and which is so absolutely perfect as to admit of no degrees or increase; for that is not the sense in which it seems to be understood by the sacred writers, but rather as importing *a prevailing and satisfactory conclusion;* a state in which the mind sees no reason to question its sincerity and safety. Nor is it necessary to this blessed condition that the person who enjoys it, should be able or disposed to use bold, strong, confident affirmation, such as, "I am as certain I am a child of God, as if a voice from heaven declared it; and as sure of arriving safely in glory at last as if I were already there." Many a modest humble believer, if the question were put to him, "Are you a child of God?" would, perhaps, under the influence of meekness and self-abasement, shrink from the positive, "I am, I am sure I am;" and content himself with saying, "I hope and believe I am, having no serious reason to doubt it, for I am deeply convinced of my fallen, sinful state; I renounce every ground of dependance, but the righteousness of Christ, and rest my hope of salvation on him. My faith has given me peace, and led me to love God. And, conscious of this, I doubt not I have passed from death unto life." This latter is the language of Scriptural assurance.

Such a prevailing and satisfactory conclusion as to our state *may be obtained.* Had no injunction in reference to it been given in the Scripture, nor any declaration made concerning it, still it might have been fairly presumed, that a change so great as that of regeneration could not have taken place without being its own evidence, to him in whom it is wrought. The old and the new nature, the work and image of Satan and of God, are not so like each other as not to be easily distinguished; but, in fact, we ARE commanded to give all diligence to obtain and preserve the full assurance of hope; and evidences are laid down by which we may ascertain whether we are the children of God or not. Every one of us may know this; the means of judging are within the reach of us all.

If, then, we *may* know it, we *ought* to know it. Assurance is in one sense our duty, as well as our privilege. If it is our duty to believe, it is our duty to hope, and if to hope at all, to hope even to assurance. Every man ought to know his spiritual condition. It is a matter of too great moment to be suffered to remain undecided. We ought not to be content to remain another hour in ignorance of our spiritual state.

How is assurance to be obtained? This is a most momentous question. May God preserve me from error in giving an answer to it. It is said by the apostle, "The Spirit itself beareth witness with our spirit, that we are the children of God." Rom. viii. 16. Now as it is witnessed, or testified by the Spirit, that we are the children of God, we naturally ask, in what manner is this testimony borne? This must either be in the way of a direct revelation to our mind, or by enabling us, on a comparison of the Spirit's work in the heart, with the description of the Spirit's work in the Word, to draw the conclusion that we are truly born again. Some believe that there is granted to each regenerated soul a direct witness, in the way of suggestion, or impression, of its spiritual birth. This, however, does not appear to me to be the meaning of the apostle. It does not accord with the context, which is obviously practical, and speaks of the influence of the Spirit as received for mortification of sin, and for the productions of all the dispositions and habits of the Christian life, especially the Spirit of adoption; it is unsupported by any other passage where assurance is spoken of; it would, if this were its meaning, come under the head of a revelation from God, and seem to require something else to authenticate it; it would open a door for mistake and self-deception; it has never been received by multitudes who have been sincerely and eminently pious, and it is unnecessary, because, without being supported by the inferential evidence, it is not to be trusted. It is much safer and more correct to consider the witness of the Spirit as purely inferential. The case stands thus: "The Holy Spirit speaks in the Word. The same Spirit operates in the heart. There must be a correspondence between his testimony in the Word, and his operation in the heart. The evidence lies in this correspondence. We take the divine Word as dictated by the Spirit, and containing a declaration of his mind—we see there what he testifies—we see especially the description which he there gives of of the faith and character of God's children—of the principles and dispositions, the affections and desires, the hopes and fears, and the peculiar walk and conversation by which they are distinguished. If *our* spirits in the court of conscience, and before the Father of our spirits, bears witness to a correspondence between this description, and what has been effected in us by the same Divine Agent, then there is a concurrence of the testimonies; the testimony of God's Spirit and the testimony of our spirits agree; the one witnesseth with the other. What the Spirit of God has wrought in us harmonizes with what the Spirit of God testifies in the Word; and in proportion as our spirits have the inward consciousness of this harmony, do we possess the witness of the Spirit to our being the children of God."*

This is in strict accordance with what is said in other places of Scripture. "These things," says the apostle John, "have I written unto you that believe on the name of the Son of God, that ye may know that ye have eternal life." 1 John, v. 13. We are to *know* that we have eternal life, by the evidence of what is *written*, and of course by the comparison of our heart and life with it.

In reply then to the question, how you may know that you are a child of God, I answer, by consciousness, and a comparison of your state with the Word of God. The apostle says, "We are all the children of God by faith in Jesus Christ," Gal. iii. 26. "I am conscious," says an assured Christian, "that I *do* believe, and therefore I know I am a child of God." And suppose he were in any doubt about the reality of his *faith*, he pursues the subject and says, "The Word of

* Dr. Wardlaw on Assurance, p. 104.

God says, in whom believing we rejoice; I *have* peace and joy. To them that believe he is precious; Christ *is* precious to *me*. Faith worketh by love: *I* love God, Christ, his people, and holiness. This is the victory that overcometh the world, even our faith; *I* have overcome the world. We know that we have passed from death unto life, because we love the brethren; I love the brethren — therefore I conclude I am a child of God. The fruits of my faith which I discern in myself, answer to the description of them given in the Word."

It is not, then, by any such methods as by dreams, or the suggestions of texts of Scripture to the mind, or visions, or impressions upon the mind, or strong persuasions of our eternal election, that we are to obtain this blessed hope of personal interest in the mercies of redemption, but by comparing our hearts with the Word of God. I will here quote the beautiful language of the celebrated Ralph Cudworth, in a sermon preached before the House of Commons during the Commonwealth: "The way to obtain a good assurance of our title to heaven, is not to climb up to it by a ladder of our own ungrounded persuasions, but to dig as low as hell by humility and self-denial in our own hearts: and though this may seem the farthest way about, yet it is indeed the nearest and safest way to it. We must, as the Greek epigram speaks, '*ascend downward*, and *descend upward*,' if we would indeed come to heaven, or get any true persuasion of our title to it. The most triumphant confidence of a Christian riseth safely and surely on this low foundation, that lies deeper under ground, and there stands firmly and steadfastly. When our heart is once turned into a conformity with the Word of God, when we feel our will to concur with his will, we shall then personally perceive a spirit of adoption within ourselves, teaching us to say, *Abba, Father.* We shall not then care for peeping into the hidden records of eternity, to see whether our names be written there in golden characters: no, we shall find a copy of God's thoughts concerning us written in our own breasts. There we may read the characters of his favor toward us: there we may feel an inward sense of his love to us, flowing out of our hearty and unfeigned love to him. And we shall be more undoubtedly persuaded of it, than if one of those winged watchmen above, that are privy to heaven's secrets, should come and tell us that they saw our names enrolled in those volumes of eternity."

In this way, and, as it appears to me, in this way only, is our personal interest in the blessings of salvation to be ascertained. It will be evident then, that our assurance will be more or less full, according to the measure of our piety. It admits of degrees of certainty, and these will be regulated by our degrees of vital, experimental godliness. Hence the force of the apostolical exhortation, *to give all diligence* to make our calling and our election sure: *i. e.*, sure to ourselves, as a clear and well-attested fact, that we are called according to the purpose of God.

It is an unquestionable fact, that many professors have not yet attained to this comfortable persuasion of their personal interest in Christ. Various reasons may be assigned for this. Some ought not to have it, for they are professors *only*, and not partakers of divine grace. In them it would be only a lie in their right hand; and crying peace, peace, when they have no right to peace. Others are kept in doubt by physical obstructions to joy and hope: they are constitutionally gloomy and dejected. Little can be said to them but to encourage them, if they are walking consistently, to endeavor to distinguish between disordered nerves, and destitution of piety; to hope against hope; and, if possible, to increase their joy by the improvement of their health. It is dangerous advice, in most cases, to let our friends judge for us of so important a matter as our spiritual condition and safety; but in the case of those to whom I am now alluding, the opinion of enlightened and judicious Christians, who think favorably of the state of the dejected, should have weight. Others, though not constitutionally depressed, are timid, hesitating and anxiously cautious; and even in common matters, find it difficult sometimes to decide an important question. This oscitancy they carry into their religious matters, and are afraid of coming to the conclusion that they are Christians, lest, after all, they should deceive themselves. To their timorous minds it seems a kind of presumption for *them* to conclude that they are the children of God: a rash and unauthorized decision, from which they start back with trepidation and alarm. They view it merely in the light of a privilege which is granted to a favored few, but not an attainment within the reach of all, or a duty, the obligation to which all ought to feel. How mistaken a view is this of the whole subject. It might surely be presumed that in every case of real scriptural piety, the subject of it would be able to ascertain his condition; that no child in the family of God need be ignorant of his divine relationship. It must strike us as very strange that a renovation of character so great as that effected in regeneration, should take place, and the recipient of it be unable to certify it. It cannot, therefore, be an unauthorized state of mind for any real and consistent Christian to arrive at, to know his heavenly birth, but what he *should* attain. Some, I fear, actually nourish doubts and fears as a mark of grace, and an evidence of humility, and consider themselves in a more secure and salutary state for questioning their safety, than concluding upon it. If, indeed, they have not the evidence of true conversion, they *ought* to doubt, or ought rather to be assured that they are not Christians; but I am now supposing the case of some good people, who, with the marks of true grace, and a consistent walk, are cherishing the error that it is safer to doubt than to decide. This is a sad mistake and a proof of deplorable ignorance of the Word of God.

Others are engaged in a microscopic analysis of their feelings, and vary their opinion of their state with every vicissitude of their emotions. A little more or a little less fluency in prayer; a greater or a less degree of enjoyment of a sermon; a higher or lower measure of elasticity of the animal spirits, produced by physical causes, raises or depresses their hopes, elevating them to confidence, or sinking them to despondency. Their opinions of their state are, therefore, in a state of perpetual vacillation. Their religious enjoyment is at the mercy of circumstances, over which they can exercise no control, and they are strangers to settled peace. If such persons would look less to themselves and more to Christ, they would be far happier. In some instances this propensity to be ever poring into the heart, is the remains of self-righteousness, leading them to look for comfort in themselves, rather than to Christ. Let them, by a calm, sober, impartial examination of their habitual past conduct, come to a conclusion of their state, and not suffer that conclusion to be disturbed by every little variation of their feelings. Neither our character nor our safety is altered, or endangered, by all those minute changes of emotion which are ever going on in the heart of a believer. A man does not doubt that he is alive, or in general good health, every time his appetite is less keen, or his sleep less sound than usual nor does he doubt the sincerity of his affection for his wife and children every time there is a less vivid sense of it than at other seasons. If in either case the symptoms of declension remain or increase, and are attended with other signs of decay, he has cause to take alarm. Thus should it be with believers as to those passing varieties of frame which occur in the experience of the holiest and the best of men. Permanent and increasing declension is alarming and should awaken doubts, but not the occasional interruption of what is denominated, by not a very felicitous expression, "*sensible comfort.*"

There is, I am persuaded, often a neglect of acknowledged duty, or the indulgence of known sin, at the bottom of those doubts and fears with which some professing Christians are troubled; some secret, beloved, and unmortified corruption, against which conscience is raising its protesting voice, but from which the subject of it refuses to part. It may be laid down as a settled point that wilful sin must lead to darkness. No sentiment can be more unscriptural, none more irrational or more shocking, than that sin should never make a believer doubt of his state; that whatever be the evils into which he falls, doubts and fears are only additions to his guilt; that all his iniquities have been atoned for in the blood of Christ, and that therefore no sin should at any time trouble his spirit, or darken the light of his joy. This is the most monstrous and miserable of all delusions." The man who comes to assurance, and maintains it, while his conscience testifies of him that he is habitually declining in religious affections, living in the habitual neglect of known duty, or in the indulgence of actual sin, is one of the most fearful instances of self-deception in our world.

But there is still another class of professing Christians, who must confess, if they are asked, that they are strangers to this assured hope of eternal life, and it is a very large class too: I mean those whose piety, if admitted to be sincere, is so low and so lukewarm, as to yield but equivocal testimony to the reality of their heavenly birth. Swallowed up in business, personal or public; immersed in politics, national or municipal; or devoted to worldly ease and domestic enjoyment, they are living sadly below their principles, privileges, and professions. Who can wonder that *they* know little of the blessedness of a persuasion that they are interested in the great salvation. As a general description of their state of mind, I should say they take it for granted they are Christians; assume that they are born from above, and with this vague, unsustained, and careless conclusion, pass on. But as to the sweet and consolatory influence deduced from premises cautiously examined, that they are the children of God, and have no reason to doubt the momentous and delightful fact, they know nothing of this; and hence when taken off from their usual pursuits, and shut up in the chamber of sickness, or laid upon the bed of death, how dark is their mind, how numerous and agitating are their doubts and fears, how distressing their solicitude! It will not do, in such circumstances, to take it for granted, and assume, without examination, that they are Christians; they must have it proved, and they now call for evidence, and alas, how little can they find! They pore into their hearts, they scrutinize their conduct, and sometimes *hope* they can discern the marks of the Spirit's work, the characters of regeneration, but, like a worn-out inscription, they are scarcely discernible, much less clearly legible. Habitual worldly-mindedness has almost effaced those holy and heavenly dispositions which are the superscriptions of God's hand upon the human heart.

Now then, my dear friends, let me earnestly admonish you to comply with the apostolic injunction, and give all diligence to the full assurance of hope unto the end. It cannot be obtained *without* diligence. There is a faith so strong, a love so fervent, and a hope so lively, that they prove their own existence, both to those who possess them, and to those who observe them. Shining substances need no other evidence of their existence than their own radiance. A man in full health needs no examination to demonstrate to him that he is alive and well; he is conscious of it, for he feels it. So should it be with a Christian. Self-examination for the purpose of ascertaining whether or no he *is* a Christian, should be unnecessary for a child of God. But then, in order to this, his religion must be in a high state of vigor and prosperity. He must ever remember the great design of the gospel, which is to establish a God-like frame and disposition of spirit, which consists in righteousness and true holiness in the hearts of men. "The grace of God that bringeth salvation, hath appeared unto all men, teaching us, that denying ungodliness and worldly lusts, we should live soberly, righteously, and godly, in this present world; looking for that blessed hope, and the glorious appearing of our great God and Savior Jesus Christ, who gave himself for us, that he might redeem us from all iniquity, and purify unto himself a peculiar people, zealous of good works." Titus ii. 11–15. From this passage it is evident the design of Christ in coming into our world, was not only to cast over us the purple robe of his righteousness, and hide our wickedness and deformity from the eye of God's avenging justice, but also, like a good physician, to cure our moral diseases: and then may we be assured of our being in a state of salvation, when we are at once conscious of a simple faith in his righteousness, and equally conscious of the spirit of holiness in our hearts, and the beauties of holiness in our character; and "the least inward lust, willingly continued in, will be like a worm fritting the gourd of our confidence, and presumptuous persuasion of God's love, and always gnawing at the root of it; and though we strive to keep it alive, and continually besprinkle it with some dews of our own, yet it will be always dying and withering in our bosoms. But a good conscience will be always a cordial to a Christian's heart: it will be softer to him than a bed of down, and he may sleep securely on it in the midst of raging and tempestuous seas, when the winds bluster, and the waves beat around him. A good conscience is the best looking-glass of heaven, in which the soul may see God's thoughts and purposes concerning it, as so many shining stars reflected from it." *Hereby we know Christ: hereby we know that Christ loves us, if we keep his commandments.*

The end of the gospel is to make us holy, happy, and useful; and assurance contributes to all these. Hope is a purifying grace, while despair is unholy, both in its nature, and in its tendency. He who has the most confident persuasion of his being a Christian now, and of his going on to heaven hereafter, and whose confidence rests on good ground, will be the holiest man. His assurance, sustained by holiness, will increase that which supports it.

And then need I prove to you that assurance is the means of happiness? The gospel is a system of joy, as its name imports: it was thus announced by the angels at the birth of Christ, "behold I bring you glad tidings of great joy;" it is thus recognised by the apostle, when he says, "the kingdom of God is righteousness, peace, and joy in the Holy Ghost." This is implied, when we are so emphatically called upon "to rejoice in the

Lord;" all of which seem to import that the genuine right temper and frame of a truly Christian mind and spirit, may be evidently concluded to be an habitual joyfulness, prevailing over all the other sources of human delight, and all the temporary causes of sorrow that occur in the world. I want you to enter deeply into this view of Christianity. I am anxious for you to be made happy by your religion. I am desirous that, as you travel to heaven, you should go on your way rejoicing: that in prosperity you should have a higher and holier source of enjoyment than providential favors; and in adversity a spring of happiness, when the cup of earthly comfort has been dashed from your lips. This is to be found in assurance. Blessed state, to be a child of God, and to know it too! to be going to heaven, and know it too! to be an heir of glory, and have evidence of the fact! Well might the poet say —

When I can read my title clear
  To mansions in the skies,
I bid farewell to every fear,
  And wipe my weeping eyes.

What sorrow need depress us; what care waste us; what danger appal us; what loss distress us, if assured of an interest in the blessing of salvation! The man assured of heaven may look at poverty, sickness, and persecution, without dismay, yea, may smile in the face of death. Assurance has enabled the dying Christian to step without shrinking, into the cold dark waters of Jordan;

confessors to sing in their dungeons, and martyrs to exult at the stake.

Be, then, diligent to make your calling and election sure. If you *are* Christians, you may know and ought to know it. Be satisfied with nothing less. Pray for it, pray earnestly, constantly, believingly. Beseech the Spirit of God to work all his works in you, and then to shine upon his own work, and enable you to draw the conclusion, that you are indeed a child of God, an heir of heaven.

No. V.

PRACTICAL RELIGION MUST BE SEEN IN EVERYTHING.

My dear Friends. It appears to me that many persons are far too limited in their ideas of the nature, design, and extent of practical religion. An individual upon being reproached for some dishonorable transaction in business as inconsistent with religion, replied, "*What has religion to do with business?*" The answer demonstrated either his ignorance, or wickedness, or both. But, if we may judge from their conduct, this is the sentiment of many professors, although, perhaps, they would not avow it. Are they not acting as if religion *had* nothing to do either with business, with temper, or with our domestic and social relations? As if it were a mere matter of opinion, devotion, or ceremony: a thing of the cloister, the closet, or the sanctuary, which is to be confined to its own retreats, and never to be allowed to approach the scenes of worldly business, and secular pursuits: a rule to direct us how we are to behave ourselves in the house of God, and to regulate our worship; and which, having done this, has accomplished its object! Is not this, I say, the view which if we may judge by their behavior, many take of religion? But can anything be more inaccurate?

Religion is a permanent, all-pervading, unchanging principle, possessing a kind of universality of nature. It must go with us, not only into the sanctuary of God, or into the closet of private devotion, but into *all* places: it must regulate our conduct, not only toward the *church*, but toward the *world:* it must operate upon us and influence us, not only on sabbath, sacramental, and fast days, but at *all* times: and must dictate, not only how we pray, and read the Bible, and keep holy the Lord's-day, but how we buy, and sell, and get gain. Religon has no exclusive time, or place, or sphere, of its own, but is a matter of all times, places, and scenes. Though heavenly in her origin, her nature, and her destiny, she is not so purely ethereal as to turn away from the scenes of this low diurnal sphere, as beneath her notice and unworthy of her control. "Wisdom crieth without; she uttereth her voice in the streets; she crieth in the chief places of concourse, in the opening of the gates; in the city she uttereth her words. Prov. i. 20.

The subject, then, of the present address is this, "*Practical religion must be seen in everything.*"

Consider your situation. You are united with society by various ties, and have corresponding duties to discharge, every one of which affords an opportunity for the exercise of religious principle. A man can as truly, though not as publicly and impressively, show his regard to principle and conscience, in the least transaction of a secular nature, as at the martyr's stake. The various claims of society afford as correct a test of moral feeling, as the claims of the church of God. Religion must be co-extensive, not only with our whole nature as constituted of body and soul, and as speaking, thinking, feeling, acting agents, but with all our relations to the world around us.

Dwell upon the commands of God. Take only two or three of these. What can be more explicit than the summary of the moral law, which is given by Christ, in supreme love to God, and equal love to man. The second is as obligatory as the first, and love to man in all the varieties of its operations and manifestations, down to the most minute offices for his comfort, is as essentially a part of religion, as love to God. Read also the apostle's comprehensive and beautiful exposition of this precept: "Love worketh no ill to his neighbor; therefore love is the fulfilling of the law." Rom. xiii. 10. How explicit and minute is the direction given in Phil. iv. 8. Whatsoever things are true, honest, just, pure, lovely, and of good report, think on these things. Observe, all these virtues relate to our conduct toward our fellow-creatures; and because there are some things we owe them which can be scarcely classified under any one of these particulars, the apostle puts in the general and delightful adjuncts, whatsoever things are "*lovely*," and of "*good report.*" And how impressive is the word, so frequently expressed in the passage, "*whatsoever* things;" as if he had said, "all that is or can be imagined to be claimed on the ground of justice, honesty, truth, purity; everything which by common opinion is thought to be amiable, attractive, honorable, and praiseworthy, let this be done by those who bear the name of Christ." To this we may add one more passage, than which nothing can be said or thought of as more imperative on a professor, to let his religion shine out in everything: "Whether ye eat, or drink, or whatsoever ye do, do all to the glory of God." 1 Cor. x. 31.

It is apparent, then, that God has taken our conduct — not only in the church, but in the world; not only in the sanctuary, but in the place of worldly business; not only to our Christian brother, but to our unconverted neighbor; not only in our devotional, but our ordinary transactions — under his direction, and made it our duty to let our religion be seen in all.

It may be useful if I here point out those matters from which professors of godliness are too apt to exclude their religion, or in which, at any rate, they are not sufficiently careful to let it appear. They are ordinarily not deficient in their sabbath-day duties: they are regular in their attendance upon the services of the sanctuary; they are constantly present, and apparently devout at the sacramental table; they are perhaps often, or always to be found at prayer-meetings or weekly-sermons; they keep up family-prayers; they subscribe money to public institutions for the spread of the gospel; they *imagine* that they are spiritually and heavenly-minded — but still there are some other parts of their conduct, in which their religion does not appear as it ought to do, nor is it any part of their care that it should, I mean their conduct toward their neighbor and each other. You observe that all these points, in which I have supposed them to be attentive to their duties, relate to their conduct toward God: they are all matters of devotion. But devotion is only a part of religion; love to our neighbor, as we have already considered, is as truly a part of religion as love to God. Now it is really the case that there are many, who though very seemingly diligent in reference to the latter, are far too remiss in reference to the former. They attach great importance to spirituality, and heavenly-mindedness, at least, they talk much about them, but they are very lax in regard to some other things, which are as much their duty, as these more elevated and unearthly states of mind. Devotion is with them everything, but morality, in its higher, and more delicate, and refined character, is but lightly spoken of: *they* love God, but leave others, whom they are pleased to denominate legal, to love their neighbor. These persons are generally known by a peculiar taste in regard to preaching. The only sermons they relish, are those which are full of *comfort;* which are addressed exclusively to the children of God; and which are of such a kind, as rather to excuse their imperfections, and make them happy in the indulgence of their corruptions, than to lead them on to higher degrees of sanctification. The enforcement of duty of any kind, even to God, is not a very welcome subject, but duty to man, is all legality and bondage.

One matter which religion claims to regulate, but from which it is excluded by many persons, is our TEMPER. If any one should be disposed to ask, "What has religion to do with temper?" I will answer this question, by referring him to the thirteenth chapter of the first epistle to the Corinthians. The whole of this exquisitely beautiful portion of divine truth, refers to temper; and it is really very solemn to consider how imperatively and essentially necessary to salvation, the Holy Spirit makes the exercise of a good temper. The most splendid miracles, the most profound knowledge of sacred truths, the most consummate eloquence in recommending them, the expenditure of a fortune in supporting them, and the martyr's death in attesting them, will, we are told, be of no avail to any one, if he have not the good temper there described. Nothing is religion in the absence of love; nothing can fit us for heaven but love; the very essence of religion is love to God for his own sake, and love to man for God's sake: we are to love our neighbor for God, and God in our neighbor. Can we love our neighbor, and yet indulge in habitual passion, malice, revenge? Oh, how much dishonor is done to religion by the bad temper of its professors; by the petulance and peevishness of one, the passion of a second, the sullenness of a third, the obstinacy of a fourth, and the cherished resentment of a fifth. It is astonishing how any who habitually indulge in such dispositions, can imagine they are the children of the God of love, the followers of Him whose designation is "the Lamb," and the temples of that divine Spirit, whose symbol is a "Dove." I am aware that there is something physical in the cause of bad tempers, but they are still subject to moral control. It may be, that some find it much more difficult to restrain and manage their temper than others; and that some who take far more pains to govern their disposition, than those who are possessed of a natural amiableness, gain far less credit than the latter. The mischief and the blame lie in supposing that as bad tempers are inherent in us, their indulgence is inevitable, and therefore excusable. If this be correct, *all* sin is inevitable and excusable, for it is all inherent. If, then, you would prove your regeneration; if you would carry on the work of sanctification; if you would promote the mortification of sin; if you would not have darkness of mind, and distress of conscience; if you would not grieve your fellow-Christians, and disturb the comfort of those around you, subdue and regulate your temper. A professing Christian, red and stormy with passion, pale with anger, furious with rage, is a most unseemly spectacle. How can the love of God or man be in such a heart? But it is not merely this excess of passion which is discreditable, but the waspishness, the touchiness, the moodishness, which many display, the sensitiveness and susceptibility to offence; in short, the being *easily* offended, which so many exhibit without an effort to resist it. Your profession requires, my dear friends, a constant resistance of such dispositions: and it is one great part of religion to keep up this resistance. Your piety and principle should be ever at hand for this purpose; always nigh and ready to be applied, with all their mighty energies and motives, to suppress every rising unhallowed emotion. "Put on, therefore, as the elect of God, holy and beloved, bowels of mercies, kindness, humbleness of mind, meekness, long-suffering; forbearing one another, and forgiving one another, if any man have a quarrel against any; even as Christ forgave you, so also do ye. And above all things, put on charity, which is the bond of perfectness. And let the peace of God rule in your hearts, to the which also ye are called in one body." Col. iii. 12, 15. This is the law of Christ, the rule of your conduct, the standard of your actions, the mould of your character. How tender the language, how touching the motives, how forcible the obligations! Abjure, then, the idea that religion has nothing to do with temper; adopt the sentiment that *your temper must be governed by your religion*, and by importunate prayer, constant watchfulness, and laborious effort, seek after the meekness and gentleness of Christ.

Another scene from which many are too apt to exclude their religion, but over the whole of which it should be seen to preside, is *their worldly transactions*. Religion not only conducts on the sabbath-day to the house of God, and there says to us, "Enter into his gates with thanksgiving, and into his courts with praise;" but it also goes with us on Monday morning to the mart of business, and says to us, "Whatsoever things are true, honest, just, pure, lovely, and of good report, think on these things and practise them." Travellers tell us, that the Chinese set up the objects of their worship, not only in their temples, but in their shops. If, then, idolatrous *Pagans* place trade under the patronage and direction of religion; if *they* acknowledge that their divinities take cognizance of secular concerns; and that one part of divine service is justice to man, how much more should this be the case with *Christians!* Yes, my friends, your religion must be seen by those who know you only as tradesmen, and have no opportunity of seeing you but in the shop. It must be at hand, ready for application to all the circumstances of life, and all the transactions of business. It must stand by in all sales, bargains, and contracts; it must prevent all over-reaching undermining, and circumventing; all false depreciation of the article you wish to purchase, and overpraising that which you desire to sell; it must forbid all falsehood, fraud, and artifice; all selfishness and grinding extortion; in short, all that kind of conduct which would make others afraid to deal with you, and give the stamp and stigma to your character of a "deep one," "a hard one," or "a slippery one." It is a disgrace to professing Christians to have either of these epithets applied to *them*. *They* should be distinguished by all that is just, true, generous, and noble. They are commanded to let their light shine *before men*. Now this can only be done by being exemplary in the discharge of those duties which fall under public observation. Although those who are conversant with you, may make shrewd guesses by what they see in your outward deportment, whether you are a man of devotional feeling, yet they cannot trace you to the family altar, or to the closet of private prayer, but they can and will quickly and certainly know whether you are true and just, honest and upright, generous and trustworthy, or on the contrary, false and unjust, fraudulent and tricking, selfish and extortionate: and if they see a want of principle in your transactions, they will of course suspect a destitution of religion in your heart, and resolve the whole of your profession into disgusting and odious hypocrisy. *Let religion then be seen in your business.*

The *discharge of the duties of our social relations* is another opportunity for exhibiting the influence of religion. Its excellence must be seen and its power felt, in making a happy home, and compelling a sojourner in the family, or a spectator of it, to exclaim, "How goodly are thy tents, O Jacob, and thy tabernacles, O Israel! As the valleys are they spread forth, as gardens by the river side, as the trees of lign-aloes which the Lord hath planted, and as cedars beside the waters." Religion ought to give strength, tenderness, and sanctity, to all the ligaments of society. It should make husbands and wives more affectionate and devoted: parents more kind, judicious, and vigilant: and children more dutiful, respectful, and attentive: masters more kind and just: servants more submissive and faithful. Religion is intended to be the magistrate of the social body, and the head of the domestic circle. We should all discharge the duties of our station *piously;* doing even common things as to the Lord, and for the Lord's sake. Like the stars of heaven, we should not only shine, but each in his own sphere. If we are unamiable at home, there must be something essentially defective in our profession.

Nor is it of small importance that our profession should be consistently maintained *abroad*, as well as at home. It must, as an integral part of ourselves, go with us everywhere, and abide with us where *we* abide. We must take it as our companion in travel, as our associate in public, as our bosom and inseparable friend. They who constantly see us at home, and occasionally meet us abroad, should recognise the same unaltered and unalterable character; the same in the crowded metropolis, as in the retired village, and the same at the fashionable watering-place, as in the rural retreat.

Religion should appear in our *recreations and entertainments*, separating us from the follies and amusements of the world; allowing neither what is polluting, nor what is frivolous: not only keeping us from the theatre, the ball-room, and the public concert, but, preventing us from turning our own habitations into the resorts of fashion and the scenes of light and dissipating entertainments. If, in the seasons allotted to relaxation from worldly business, anything more be necessary than the cheerful and holy intercourse and conversation of the pious, then the beautiful scenery of nature, the works of charity, the pursuits of science, or the exercises of devotion, should be enough. A Christian should appear to be a Christian, in his lighter as well as in his graver occupations.

Nor should even our *politics* be placed beyond the control of our piety. A professor of religion has duties to discharge as a citizen, as well as a Christian, since he is a member of society at large as well as of the church: and it is a misguided sanctity, a spirit of fanaticism alone, that attempts to dissuade him from discharging the obligation he owes to the community. But then, he should act as a Christian, at the very time he is acting as a citizen. Instead of making his religion political, he should make his politics religious. It ill becomes a follower of Him whose kingdom is not of this world, to be a furious political partisan filled with hatred, malice, and all uncharitable ness, toward those who differ from him: and who would not scruple to use any means, however base, to ensure the success of his own party; nor is it less contrary to the Christian profession to be seduced from the path his conscience dictates, by the arts of corruption, or to be intimidated by the threats of power. Religion should induce a man to carry his conscience with him, as his guide and protector, into all the scenes and circumstances in which he is required to act for his country, and he should ever give his voice or his vote, as he would do, if he knew he was tc be called to account for that act the next moment, at the bar of God.

But why do I particularize? I remind you again, your religion should be seen in *everything;* in matters so great as to call for martyrdom, and so minute, as the least trifle of any single day's transactions. It does not consist, I repeat, merely of prayers, sermons, and sacraments, but of supreme love to God, and equal love to man, running out into all the endless varieties of application anu operation, of which these sacred affections are susceptible. Like the blood of our corporeal system, which does not confine itself to two or threc large arterial ducts, but warms, vitalizes, and moves the man, and pours the tide of life and the impulse of activity through a thousand vessels some of them almost too minute to be seen; so religion is the sustaining, moving principle of the whole of the *new* man, which is renewed in knowledge and true holiness, after the image of him that created him: it is not to be confined to any special places, modes, or seasons of operation, but is to diffuse itself through all the thousand little acts that are every day performed, and in the performance of which we have an opportunity, and are under obligation to glorify God.

But this is not how the matter is regarded by the generality of professing Christians, if, indeed, we may judge from their conduct; for when religion is mentioned, the only idea that many are apt to associate with that term, is the performance of devotional exercises, or the indulgence of devotional feelings; forgetting that good temper, the payment of debts, the fulfilment of contracts, the forgiveness of injuries, the duties of home, and the conscientious use of the elective franchise, are as truly a part of religion as the observance of the sabbath, or the celebration of the Lord's Supper.

And this is, in fact, the religion which the world expects of us. *They* demand of us, that we carry our religion into everything, whether *we* meet the demand or not. Do they reproach us with inconsistency only when we neglect private or public prayer? O no. What do they know or care about such matters? But when professors are passionate, revengeful, and malicious; when they are shuffling, artful, and fraudulent; when they are slippery, treacherous, and evasive; when they are unkind, unamiable, and oppressive, then they are ever ready with the taunt, "*This is your religion is it?*" By which they mean to insinuate, that those who profess to believe in Christ for salvation, ought not thus to have belied a profession which binds them to be holy in all manner of conversation. *They* never ask, "What has religion to do with business?" if professors do.

Consider how much injury has been done to the character of religion, by not taking this view of its universal dominion. One single defect has been enough, in some cases, to disparage a whole character: and one act of inconsistency, and that not a very considerable one either, has thrown its shadow over many excellences. It may be there were those who knew the individual by only that one transaction; they knew nothing of his general character, or his many valuable qualities, but they saw him in that one act from which religion was unhappily excluded, and judging from the only evidence which has come before them, they are ready to condemn him as a base designing hypocrite.

What a beauty would invest the character which derives its symmetry from the pervading influence of true piety; the character in which religion is seen giving devotion and zeal to the Christian; justice and truth to the tradesman; patriotism and loyalty to the citizen; affection to the husband; fondness to the father; gentleness to the neighbor; kindness to the master; and charity to all: in which religion regulates the whole series of words and actions, running through the whole tenor of the conduct, and dictating what is right to be done in the ten thousand little occurrences that are ever transpiring in the business of life: what a character, I say, is this, in which all the greater virtues unite with all the lesser graces, and religion is the bond that holds them together. Such a character should every professing Christian present to the world, and he is no longer consistent with his profession, than while he is holding out such a pattern of excellence to mankind.

Permit me then, my dear friends, in conclusion, to admonish you with great earnestness and solicitude, to enter into the subject of this address. While you are intent on the acquisition of more and more of that Spirituality and Heavenliness of mind, and of the Assurance of Hope, which have been the subjects of the three preceding tracts, may you be equally solicitous to "let your light shine before men, that they seeing your good works, may glorify God your heavenly Father." Remember it is not religion as it appears in some few things, nor in many, but in *all*, that will do this. There can be here no compensatory process: no setting off excellences against defects; no balancing diligence in some matters against neglect in others. Depend upon it as a fact, that a partial religion, and a little of religion, dishonor God more than none at all. "Wherefore, my beloved brethren, be ye steadfast, immoveable, always abounding in the work of the Lord, forasmuch as ye know that your labor is not in vain in the Lord. Herein is your father glorified, that you bear much fruit. Then will you not be ashamed when ye have respect unto all his commandments. Do all this without murmurings and disputings, that ye may be blameless and harmless, tne sons of God without rebuke, in the midst of a crooked and perverse nation, among whom shine ye as lights in the world; holding forth the word of life; that I may rejoice in the day of Christ, that I have not run in vain, neither labored in vain." Phil. ii. 14-16.

No. VI.

HOW TO SPEND A PROFITABLE SABBATH.

My Dear Friends: The design of the present address is to direct you "*How to Spend a Profitable Sabbath.*" How rich a boon has celestial mercy bestowed upon our laboring, toil-worn world in the day of sacred rest. What should we do, as regards either body or soul, without the sabbath, to invigorate the impaired energies of the one, and recruit the wasted piety of the other? If the man of wealth and leisure, whose time is all his own, to spend it, if it please him so to do, in reading meditation, and prayer, feels little need of such a season of repose, not so the tradesman, the servant, and the laborer. How sweet to them, as Saturday evening is closing upon them, and all the weariness of six days' labor is pressing them down, is the reflection, "To-morrow is the sabbath of the Lord." There is no need to prove to them by elaborate argumentation, that the sabbath is of perpetual obligation, for they cannot persuade themselves that He who hath loved them in Christ Jesus, would have left them without such an opportunity as this affords, in their scene of toil, to dwell upon his love, and enjoy it: and hence, and often as the season comes round, they meet its very dawn with the words of WATTS—

> "Welcome sweet day of rest,
> That saw the Lord arise —
> Welcome to this reviving breast,
> And these rejoicing eyes."

The various mental associations, equally serene and delightful — the hallowed pleasures — the recollections and anticipations — the pure immortal hopes — the rapt exercises of devotion, which, like the day-spring from on high, bless the passing hours of the sabbath, and render it the best type of heaven itself, make it a blessing to the child of God, which he would not part with for ten thousand times the gain he could acquire by devoting it to business and to wealth: and his heart would claim it as a privilege to keep holy the sabbath-day, even if his conscience did not dictate it as a duty.

If, my dear friends, you would keep up the power of godliness in your souls, if you would live by faith upon the Son of God, if you would overcome the world and set your affections upon things above, spend well your sabbaths. These are the days of the soul's gains; her golden seasons for growing rich, in all that constitutes spiritual prosperity; her times, not only for the enjoyment of devotion, but for gaining new light to guide the conscience, and fresh strength to invigorate all her religious and moral principles. Religion would retire from the world with the sabbath, and would be feeble and sickly in the church, if, indeed, it could live even there, without the aids of this holy day.

But how may our sabbaths be made profitable and pleasant to us?

1. *By a deep impression of their inestimable value, and a great anxiety to spend them well.* That which we esteem of no consequence, we shall be at no trouble to apply to any useful purpose The first way, then, to spend a profitable sabbath, is real solicitude to do so. And are you destitute of this? Taken up as you are with the cares, labors, and anxieties of the world; urged by incessant demands upon your time; distracted by various claims upon your attention by objects all around you, and worn down by labor day after day, till, if you were not too busy, you are too weary to meditate on things unseen and eternal, *ought* you not to be anxious about the improvement of your *sabbaths?* Ought you not to be *full* of desire that these days may be well spent? If they are lost to your soul's interests, nearly all time is lost, and no portion will be well employed for your eternal welfare. Professing Christians are not duly impressed, in general, with the importance of this matter. They complain how much their time and attention are occupied with this world's business through the week, and yet are not sufficiently impressed with the necessity and vast importance of spending well their sabbaths.

2. *Endeavor, as much as possible, to keep up through the days and business of the week, a spiritual frame of mind.* The great obstacle to the profit and pleasure of our sabbaths, is the intrusion of worldly thoughts and anxieties. These are the obscene birds which light upon the sacrifice, and which we find it so difficult to keep or drive away. Why is this? Just because we suffer our minds to be so deeply, I may almost say wholly, occupied by earthly pursuits during the six days of labor. It is not safe nor proper to shove out our religion from working-days, and trust entirely for its preservation to the exercises of the sabbath. We cannot easily make so sudden and entire a transition from things secular to things sacred, as to be wholly carnal and worldly up to Saturday night, and then entirely to throw off the world on Sunday morning, and be wholly spiritual through that one day. The day of devotion and the days of labor act and react upon each other; they who would keep up their piety in the week, must be diligent in cultivating it on the sabbath, and they who would successfully cultivate it on the sabbath, must not let it down very low during the days of the week. It is a fatal error, and sad delusion, for a professor to quiet his conscience, when reproaching him for his backslidings of heart, by the answer, "Sunday is coming, when I shall fetch up this lost ground."

3. *It is desirable, where it can be accomplished,*

to end the business of the week early on Saturday evening, and thus secure a portion of time for reflection and devotional exercises. Unhappily, the modern habits of trade render this all but impossible with many, who are kept hard at work till almost, if not quite sabbath morning, and then retire to rest so jaded, that they find it difficult to rise early next day for the worship of God. But where time *can* be commanded, it ought to be, and an extra half hour or hour spent in the closet on the eve of the sabbath, communing with God, the Bible, and our hearts. It was the custom of the Christians in America, at one time, to begin the sabbath at sunset on Saturday evening. This cannot and need not be done, but they who would enjoy and improve the season of holy rest, should not, if they could help it, drive business or social festivities to a late hour on Saturday evening. That evening ought not to be a visiting time, except it be such visits as would prepare the mind for sabbath occupations. Should a few pious friends in the same neighborhood determine to meet at that time for prayer and Christian communion, this would be not only proper in itself, but a useful method of preparing for the exercises of the sacred day.

4. *We must not only abstain from worldly labor on the sabbath,* if we would improve it to any spiritual purpose, *but from worldly* THOUGHTS. When the tradesman closes his shop on Saturday evening, he should lock up in it all his worldly

thoughts and anxieties, plans and purposes, not suffer any of them, if possible, to escape, to molest him on the sabbath. An eminently holy friend of mine who carried on trade in London, and lived in its environs, used to say, "He always left his business on Saturday evening on London bridge, to be taken up there again on Monday morning." This is a blessed kind of self-control, and to a considerable extent may be acquired by labor and prayer. Let the tradesman say, and try to give effect to his saying, "I will leave my business in my shop on the eve of the sabbath, and endeavor to forget on that sacred day that I *have* a business." Of course it will require great pains, but if such pains are taken, it may and will be done. Oh, how many turn the house of God into a house of merchandise, and while hearing sermons, or professedly joining in prayer, or receiving the sacramental emblems, are thinking about buying and selling, and reflecting upon the business of the past week, or making arrangements for that of the coming one! How sinful is this in the sight of God, what a detriment to religion, and an injury to the soul! If you would keep away worldly thoughts, do nothing to produce them. Never open business-letters on the sabbath, nor even have them brought to your hands. It is a great reproach for professing Christians to be seen going to the postoffice for or with their letters on the sabbath. Do not converse with others about trade and politics on the day of rest, and never touch a newspaper. Such practices turn away the mind from spiritual things, and divert the whole current of its thoughts. There can be no real communion with God, no steadfast beholding the things that are unseen and eternal, if we thus keep the world at our elbow, and place its objects before our eyes. We must endeavor, as much as possible, to divest ourselves of a secular *frame of mind*, and put on a holy, serious, and devout one. Not that we should be gloomy and sad: no, while every dream of levity, every trifling disposition, every feeling of unhallowed mirth, is suppressed, and the mind is resolutely and conscientiously directed toward religious truth and duty, the sabbath, seeing it is a feast and not a fast, and a festival of great and lasting interest, should be a day of cheerful gratitude, and of joyous thanksgiving, as becomes the auspicious season, which the great Spirit of the universe has set apart for receiving the homage of his creatures, and for ratifying his grace to the children of the dust. "It is not for Israel in the hour of hope, in the prospect, yea, the possession of redemption, to hang their harps upon the willows, as if nothing befitted their condition, but silently and in sorrow to listen to the sullen murmurs of the waters of Babylon." — "Rejoice in the Lord. Enter into his gates with thanksgivings, and into his courts with praise. Be thankful unto him and bless his name." The Christian, always cheerful, should let his joy not only be felt, but *seen* on the sabbath. If he is the head of a family, he should illumine his dwelling on that day especially, with the light of his countenance, and present to his children and his servants, who then have a nearer and better opportunity of observing what manner of man he is, the type of happiness and holiness; the gladsome spectacle of one who, in the passing hours of an earthly sabbath, realizes the emblem and the pledge of "the rest remaining for the people of God."

5. If we would spend a profitable sabbath, *we must not waste "the sweet hour of prime" in slothful indulgence upon our bed.* They who sleep away the morning till they have scarcely time to get ready for public worship, can expect no benefit, for they seek none, from the ordinances of God's house. Early rising is essential to a devotional spirit. If we secure no portion of time for private prayer before breakfast, we can rarely get any through the day. The sabbath is the last day we should allow to be abridged by lengthened slumbers. If, then, you would spend well this holy season, say, as did the Psalmist, "My heart is fixed, O God, my heart is fixed, I will sing and give praise. Awake up, my glory; awake, psaltery and harp; I myself will awake early." Awake to prayer, reading the Scriptures, and meditation. Arise to seek the favor of God. "His morning smiles bless all the day." Be found at his footstool wrestling for his grace to come upon your souls in the ordinances of religion. Can he who goes prayerless to the sanctuary expect to be

blessed in it? What right or what reason has he to look for favor from the Lord, who will not sacrifice half an hour's sleep to seek it by prayer? The slothful *Christian* can no more expect to prosper, than the slothful *tradesman*. On the other hand, what a rich communication of light, and love, and joy, might he not look for, who rises early to obtain it by supplication, and who always goes from the closet to the sanctuary.

6. If we would gain benefit by the word, *we must make our* PROFITING *the specific object of hearing it preached.* By *profiting* I mean our growth in religious knowledge, affection, and practice; in other words, the increase of our holiness, spirituality, and heavenly-mindedness. In nothing, I believe, are professing Christians more deficient than in their manner *of*, and motives *for* attending the public means of grace. It is painful and humiliating to think how extensively the gratifications of taste, and the pleasure produced by eloquence and oratory, are substituted for the cultivation of the mind in scriptural truth, and the improvement of the heart in Christian excellence. To be *pleased*, and not to be *profited*, is the object of the multitude. Hence the question, so often asked of those who have been listening to the solemn truths of salvation and eternity, "Well, how have you been *pleased* to-day?" And hence also, the common answer to such an inquiry, "O greatly delighted. It was a most eloquent sermon." Pleased we may and ought to seek to be,

but only as we are profited. Eloquence we may covet and admire; but then it should be the eloquence of truth, and not of mere rhetoric; the eloquence which makes us hate sin, love God, and mortify our corruptions; the eloquence which leaves us neither time nor disposition to praise, or scarcely think of the preacher, but absorbs us in the subject; the eloquence which burns into the very heart and consumes our lusts, and stimulates and strengthens our virtues; the eloquence of the Bible, and not of the school-book. What sabbaths we should spend, if before we left our habitations to take our seats in the house of God, we entered our closet, and, as in the presence of God, solemnly placed such questions as these to our souls: "What is, or should be my object in going to the house of God to-day? Am I going to be pleased or profited? Is it my wish to hear the preacher merely, or his Master? Is it the *manner* in which the truth is to be stated, or the *matter of the truth itself*, that I am anxious to hear? And what is now the state of my soul, and what are my wishes in reference to it? Do I want my lukewarmness to be kindled into the glow of holy love? Do I desire my corruptions to be mortified, and my languishing graces to be revived? Do I seek the conquest and eradication of some besetting sin, and am I prepared to be pleased with any sermon, though destitute of all the attractions of eloquence, that will accomplish this object?" The Christians who take this view of the end of preaching; who go to hear God's truth and not mere eloquence; who, while hearing, consider that it is God speaking to them by and through his minister; who pray while they hear, and whose prayer it is, that they might be profited; these are the persons who spend not only pleasant but improving sabbaths.

7. *Much of the improvement of our sabbaths depends on the state of our minds during what may be called the* DEVOTIONAL *exercises; I mean the prayers and the singing.* If we consider these, as too many do consider them, only supplemental and inferior parts of the service, in which we have little interest, and which require but little attention, we shall not derive much spiritual advantage from the ordinances of God's house, and the occupations of the day of rest. It is to be feared, that a sinful vagrancy of thought, which they take no pains to check, characterizes the frame of many persons during the season of prayer; and that at the very time the cloud of incense is rising before the throne of heaven, their mind is wandering to the very ends of the earth, and instead of communing with God upon the mercy-seat, they are conversing with the most trifling, perhaps, with sinful objects. The prayers, if they are such as should be presented, simple, fervent, devout; and the singing, if it be such as alone ought to be conducted in the house of God, congregational, plain, solemn, have a peculiar adaptation to give intensity to the devout feelings of the

heart, and to promote our personal piety, and those persons will profit most, who endeavor to enter deeply into all the sentiments and emotions of these parts of the worship of God.

8. In order to spend a profitable sabbath, *great care ought to be taken to improve well the interval of public worship.* It should be our aim, where the matter is within our choice, not to live at too great a distance from the sanctuary; much time is lost, much distraction of mind is produced, much weariness of mind is brought on, by not attending to this, and the mind is prevented by fatigue when it reaches the house of God from enjoying its ordinances, and by the same cause, from profitable reflection on returning home. We should not suffer the impressions produced by public worship, to be effaced by general conversation on our way to our own habitation, or around our own table. On reaching our place of abode we should seek the retirement of the closet, to recall what we have heard; to perpetuate by reflection our feelings, convictions, and purposes; and to sanctify all by prayer. Instead of wishing to indulge our appetite by a warm and plentiful dinner, in the preparation of which we have deprived our servants of *their* day of rest, we should be content with simple and cold fare, and consider the sabbath as a day rather to feast the mind, than the body. The afternoon should not be spent in lounging over the table and the wine, but partly in meditation and private prayer; partly in

catechising the children; and partly, where it can be enjoyed, in domestic psalmody and thanksgiving. Every family should be a choir, where there is a capacity for vocal music, and, in order to this, it would be desirable that singing should be more cultivated than it is. If, instead of our sons and our daughters being trained to music, merely as a drawing-room accomplishment, and for the purpose of having their simplicity corrupted, and their vanity flattered *by showing them off* before company, they were trained for domestic harmony, to what a holy and happy account might their musical talent and acquirements be turned! What harmony is *sweeter*, if that of the great congregation be *grander*, than the dulcet sounds which gladden the habitation of a pious family on the Christian sabbath, when parents and children blend their vocal and instrumental music in the praise of Almighty God, and the Lord Jesus Christ!

9. Before the day quite departs, and sleep drowns in oblivion, or only keeps alive in dreams, the solemn engagements and topics which have filled its fleeting hours, we should be found again in our closets, reviewing the whole, and pouring over all the silent and dewy influence of prayer: this being done, then taking care, as the last duty of the day, as we lay our head upon our pillow, and resign ourselves to slumber, to fall asleep with the petition, "Seal instruction upon my heart, O God, and let my profiting appear unto all men."

10. One more step should be taken, and that is, to secure a portion of time on the Monday morning before we replunge into the business, and labors, and anxieties of the world, to look back on the day that is past, for the double purpose, first, of recalling the views, emotions, and purposes, that were suggested by the services of the sanctuary, and the sabbath; and then, of settling with ourselves a plan for reducing them all to action.

There are one or two classes of Christians, who perhaps may feel that the foregoing remarks are not so applicable to them as to some others, and to whom, therefore, I would now suggest a few hints. Many Sunday School Teachers happily know by experience the value of the sabbath, but are in danger of losing something of its enjoyment, and even of its improvement, by the bustle and labors of their office. It is, I am aware, an act of self-denial, and no small sacrifice, to surrender the calm repose of the closet and the sanctuary, for the active, and sometimes harassing duties of the school-room and the class. You, my young friends, need great care, lest you lose the profit of the sabbath for yourselves, while you are seeking to render it profitable to others. Rise early in the morning for meditation and prayer, before you go to the scene of your labors. Endeavor to discharge your duties to the children in a spirit of seriousness and prayer. Avoid all trifling conversation with your fellow-teachers. Let the intervals of worship be well employed in retirement, and try as much as possible to keep your attention fixed on the sermon and the prayers in the house of God, even when seated amid your youthful charge. Endeavor, in humble dependance upon the Spirit of God, to be *useful*, and then, "in watering others, you shall yourselves be watered."

The POORER MEMBERS of the church demand a little special attention. Be you, my dear friends, peculiarly thankful for this short, sweet respite from the curse denounced on fallen man — "In the sweat of thy brow shalt thou eat bread until thou return unto the ground." Enter into God's merciful provision for your comfort, and do everything to enjoy and improve the season of rest. Let everything necessary to be done for the order, comfort, and cleanliness of the family, be finished on the Saturday evening, and even the food prepared for the sabbath's repast. Let not the husband deprive the wife of her day of repose by requiring her to give up her attendance upon public worship, or if detained at home by young children, to endure the additional privation of losing her opportunities of private and solitary devotion, in order to gratify his palate by a warm dinner. Nor should the husband refuse to take his turn in looking after the house and the young family at home, that his wife may have an opportunity to enjoy the refreshing influence of public worship, and "the communion of saints." Few persons are more to be pitied than the poor mothers of young families, who are united to husbands, that have not tenderness enough to give their wives a share of the sabbatical privilege. Let such women, amid all their privations, keep up the expectation of "the rest that remaineth for the people of God." Yes, heaven is an eternal sabbath. There the wicked cease from troubling and the weary are at rest. No domestic cares shall follow you there. No family labors or duties shall there detain you from the assembly of the saints. No ungenerous husband shall there hinder you from going to the sanctuary of God. No infirm body shall obstruct your enjoyment, or be a clog upon the spirit that would otherwise mount on the wing of devotion to God its supreme good. Eternity shall roll on, and its repose shall never be broken in upon by a single sorrow, sin, or labor: your soul shall end its weary pilgrimage, and lie down to rest for ever in the presence of God, where there is fulness of joy, and at his right hand where there are pleasures for evermore.

In such manner, my dear friends, we may spend our sabbaths upon earth both pleasantly and profitably: and spend them in the prospect and hope of a heavenly and eternal one, and in preparation for its exalted services, and its complete felicity. The sun of that day shall never set; its holy convocation shall never break up; and its services never know a termination, an interruption, or intermission. "Remember therefore the sabbath-day to keep it holy."—"Let its high and sacred character be ever present to your minds, persuaded that it was appointed for no trivial purposes—that if there are benefits of a subordinate nature to be derived from it, such as the respite afforded by it, from the labors of the week, these are not its most noble distinctions; but that it is an institution founded by a mandate of the Deity to secure from oblivion the most momentous facts, and to exist throughout all generations, a memento of the creation of the world by the power of God, and the salvation of man by the death of Christ. Let the day, therefore, which testifies to the world that God is righteous, powerful, and good; and that man is redeemed, and immortal, be spent in a manner correspondent with these stupendous facts.'

No. VII.

CHRISTIAN OBLIGATIONS

My Dear Friends: "She did what she could." Such was the testimony borne by Christ to Mary, the sister of Lazarus, when she poured upon his sacred person her alabaster-box of precious ointment. Mark xiv. 1-9. What an eulogium! And from such lips too! Blessed woman! unknown, perhaps, beyond the boundaries of her own village, little did she imagine, when she was filling the room with the perfume of her unguent, that she was performing an act which would fill the world with the fragrance of her memory. How much greater the honor of anointing Jesus to his burial, in one of the humblest cottages of Bethany, than to be anointed upon the proudest throne that ever glittered with the gold of Ophir. So true is it that piety immortalizes its subject, and invests every one who practises it with a deathless renown. Such was the ardor of this woman's love and gratitude to her Savior, that, in order to express her emotions, she ventured to the very verge of the rules of decorum, and, disregarding the curious eyes and censorious tongues of both the host and his guests, she lavished her box of precious ointment upon the body of her Lord. Yes, it was ove *to* Christ that prompted this act, and the love *of* Christ to this daughter of Abraham, which bestowed upon her the token of his gracious approbation, which is to be seen and read by all men. Whether he meant, as in the case of the poor widow, she gave *all* she had, or simply, that regardless of the cost of the ointment, and without stopping to examine whether she could afford it or not, she brought it as the highest testimonial she could give of her love to Christ, and of her desire to honor him to the extent of her power, it is of no consequence to inquire; in either case, it was a costly expression of the purest and the strongest affection.

This act of MARY suggests a series of evangelical remarks, and of consecutive and important queries.

All true believers are under infinite obligations to Christ. Take your station at the cross in the hour and scene of his redeeming agony, and hear the voice which asks: "How much owest thou thy Lord?" Thence go and place yourselves in imagination on the borders of the bottomless and flaming pit whence he has delivered you, still followed by the question, "How much owest thou thy Lord?" And then ascend to the celestial city, and with all its honors, and felicities spread around you, once more hear the voice, 'How much owest thou thy Lord?"

A Christian's soul ought ever to be filled with a sense of his obligations to Christ, and fired with the love and gratitude they should inspire. In his history there should be no seasons of forgetfulness, or of coldness toward the Lord that bought him, but he should be constrained always, by the love of Christ.

His love to the Saviour *should ever prompt the inquiry: "What shall I render unto the Lord for all his benefits toward me."* If in a right state of mind, he is not content with the inquiry: "What shall I *feel;* or what shall I *say* for Christ; but what shall I *do?*" Love is practical, and so is gratitude. It is more, it is diligent, laborious, ingenious, self-denying. If we love a friend, or feel grateful to a benefactor, we ask ourselves, and ask others, what we can do to please him. We get a knowledge of his tastes, wishes, predilections, and then *do* something that we suppose will be pleasing, welcome, and acceptable to him. Thus MARY acted. She looked round on her little possessions, with the question, "What can I do or give to my Lord." The alabaster-box caught her eye, and she exclaimed: "It is precious and costly; and for that very reason he shall have it." So should the Christian act.

Having found out what he *can* do, and what he imagines will be acceptable to Christ, *he should promptly and cheerfully do it,* however laborious, self-denying, or expensive it may be. "Oh what has he not given to me?" he exclaims, "his life, his death; his cradle, his cross; his agony, and bloody sweat; and what can I withhold from him?"

Everything a Christian does for Christ, should be done from a pure principle of love and gratitude. Nothing should be done from vanity or a regard to fame; nothing from pride and ostentation; nothing from self-righteousness: nothing from compulsion; but all from love, and gratitude, and conscience.

I make one more remark, and it is, *that there is always, and especially in this age, ample opportunity for a Christian to show, by substantial acts, his love to Christ.* It is true Christ is no longer upon earth going about doing good, and therefore we cannot now open to him our door, spread for him the table, make for him a feast, or anoint his head with precious ointments; but though he has ascended on high, he has left behind him two representatives—*His members,* and *His cause.* In reference to the former, he has most explicitly told us, that "whatever we do unto the least of them," he takes as done unto himself. Matthew x. 40–42; xxv. 35–45. All Christians have an opportunity of doing something for Christ in the way of comforting his sorrowful, relieving his necessitous, or restoring his backsliding disciples. Brotherly love is love to Christ. And it is not, perhaps, sufficiently considered by professing Christians, what an emphatic expressions this is, of our attachment to the Savior, or how kind he takes it of us, to act kindly toward his people. If a mother considers every act of favor shown to her child as shown to herself, how much more does Christ regard the benefits bestowed upon his people as bestowed upon *him;* for what is a mother's love to that of a Savior's?

But beside the members of his mystical body, Christ is also represented upon earth by *his cause.* The cause of true religion is the cause of Christ: its doctrines speak of *him*, its precepts refer to *him*, its institutes commemorate *him*. He is the end and object of all. This cause is promoted in various ways; by the preaching of the gospel, and of course the education of preachers; by the support of Christian missions; by the circulation of the Scriptures and religious tracts; by the education of children and adults; and numerous other methods. Whatever means are employed to diffuse the knowledge and promote the influence of true religion, if done from love to Christ, is of course an expression of attachment to him.

It is evident, therefore, that every Christian *can do something for Christ.* No individual is so poor, so illiterate, so obscure, as to have no opportunity of performing any substantial acts of service for the Redeemer. God has not placed a single disciple in a situation, where nothing can be done for Christ. Some have more opportunities than others; but *all* have some opportunity. To one is given ten talents, to others five, and to all besides, one. There is no monopoly of the honor of doing good; no chartered company of philanthropists; no patentees of mercy. To do something for spreading he cause of Christ, as a *duty*, is binding on every man's conscience, and every woman's too; and, as a *privilege*, is within the reach of every one's desire. The peasant and the mechanic; the man-servant and the maid-servant; the pauper and the cripple, may all do something for the Lord Jesus. If they cannot give pound they can give pence; if they cannot influence and move a multitude, they can, perhaps, influence some individual; if they have not great abilities, they have some. No, none that love Christ can honestly say, he has given them no opportunity to serve his cause. Take the case of a laboring man, and see in how many ways even *he* can act for Christ: he can train up his children in the fear of God; set an example of religion to his neighbors; persuade some that neglect the house of God to accompany him to public worship; rebuke the sinner in his ways; subscribe his own penny, and gather the pence of others for a religious society; distribute religious tracts; visit the sick to talk and pray with them: all these things he can do, and others which a little ingenuity can invent for his own peculiar situation.

I want to take from every one the dead weight of helplessness and uselessness, which hangs about them to depress and discourage them, and to excite a holy and laudable sense of their just importance, and that there is some post for them to occupy, and some work for them to do in our world. In every manufactory there is something for the child, as well as the adult; and in every machine something for the least pin, as well as the flywheel, to do. None are useless, nothing is superfluous. This is encouraging, and at the same time stimulating to the poor, for whom I write, as well as for the rich. Jesus Christ has given a duty to every man, and expects every man to *do* his duty. God's voice says: "A great work is to be done on the earth. Do something. All do it. Do something, do it." Let no man reply, "*I* can do *nothing*."

I now go on to propose a series of consecutive and important questions. *What* HAVE *you done for Christ?* What have you done compared with your obligations, your opportunities, your professions? Look back upon your life and course of action; examine your creed; consider what you have professed to Christ and before the world; recollect all the opportunities of usefulness that God has thrown in your way; calculate the resources he has placed at your disposal; and then ask yourselves the solemn question: "What have I *done?*" Look at what others have done, with, perhaps, far less opportunity or ability than you, and again ask the question: "What have *I* done?" Sum it all up, and what does it amount to? Is there a soul in heaven, or in the way to it, whom *you* have sent there? Have you made any *direct effort* to save a soul? What have you done in the way of property, exertion, influence, compared with what you might have done, and should have done?

What ARE *you* NOW *doing for Christ?* What course or scheme of usefulness does this address find you pursuing? What institution points to you as one of its active and liberal supporters? What plan of modern benevolence, and Christian enterprise is indebted to you for counsel, property, labor, and time, and regards you as one of its main pillars? Where are you, in what part of the great field of the world are you working, and what work are you doing? Perhaps you say: "I love to work alone, and am not fond of these confederations." Very well. Choose your own way of doing good, so as you do it. What then are the objects of your silent and solitary benevolence, and the channels through which you are pouring the streams of your mercy?

What CAN *you do?* This is a most momentous question, and should neither be dismissed hastily, nor answered carelessly. It requires great seriousness of inquiry, diligence of investigation, and cautiousness of research; and, moreover, much self-knowledge, modesty, and impartiality. "Can,' and "cannot," are small, frequently-repeated, and seemingly very insignificant words; but, in reality, they are immensely important, and ought not to be pronounced in haste or in levity. When we say "*cannot*," energy is paralyzed, and effort is suspended. We have pronounced a thing to be impossible, and who attempts impossibilities? Let us be cautious how we say "*cannot*." When we say "*can*" we become responsible, for this little monosyllable measures our accountability. We then utter a word which should be followed by action. What then *can* you do for Christ? Inquire, examine, study, and pray for light. Investigate your circumstances, situation, abilities, resources, opportunities. Perhaps you have property, yet but little talent for speaking; well, give, then, and give the more from the consideration that you cannot do anything else. Give what you *can*, and beware how you limit what you can give. Think *how much* you can give, not how little. Remember God knows what you can give. Look round upon your property with the word "can" upon your lips. But perhaps you have not much property, but you have ability to influence others. Employ it, then, exert it to the uttermost, and the more because you have no wealth of your own to give. It may be you have talents for speaking; well, speak, then, for Christ, not for self under the impulse of vanity, but for *Christ.* Or you have a tact for business; then go to committees, and act there humbly, laboriously, unostentatiously. You are young, and can employ yourself as a Sunday school teacher; go, without delay, to this scene of useful occupation. Or you can distribute tracts, or read the Scriptures to the poor, or collect moneys; do it, then. But it is needless for me to enumerate and specify, if you will but take up the question: "*What can I do?*" If there be but a sincere desire to do something, and to do all you can, ingenuity would soon come to your help, and you would be astonished to find out what and how much you can do. Do not say, "What can *others* do?" but "What can *I* do?" nor, "What could *I* do if others would do their duty?" but, "What can *I* do by myself and without them?"

What OUGHT *you to do?* Here is another important word, "*ought.*" This is the rule of duty: it means all a man can do, and will be condemned for not doing. To the question, what ought you to do, I answer: "All you can do." This is demanded by Christ. And he set you the example, for he did all he could for your salvation. Conscience, gratitude, justice, love, demand it of you.

What WILL *you do?* What from this hour will you determine to do? Will the past effort satisfy you? *Does* it satisfy you? What, have you done enough for Christ? Stop before you answer that question. Let me take you again to the cross, to the borders of the pit, to the world of glory, and, in sight of those stupendous scenes, let me ask you: "Have you done enough for Him who *thus* loved you?" What should satisfy the man, as the sum total of his efforts for Christ, who knows and feels that he owes his deliverance from eternal torment, and his salvation to eternal glory, to his amazing and unutterable love? What *will* satisfy him? Begin afresh from the reading of this address, to study your obligations to Christ; to fathom the depth of misery from which he has delivered you; to measure the height of glory to which he is advancing you, and all by his dear cross, and then inquire by what new and more emphatic way you shall testify your love to Christ; by what new scheme of usefulness you shall seek to express the sense you bear of his sovereign and amazing love. Go afresh to him with the prayer of the converted SAUL, and say to him: "*Lord, what wilt thou have me to do?*" And wait and watch for the answer.

What would be the result if all professing Christians did what they could? What a mass of wealth, of intellect, and of energy, remains yet unemployed for Christ, not only in the world, but also in the church. How many of his professed disciples are doing comparatively nothing; how many more but a little; and how few can even approximate to the eulogy of MARY, and deserve the honor of having it said of them: "They did what they could." Were all to begin seriously to study, and diligently and prayerfully to employ their resources, for the glory of the Savior in the spread of his cause, what might not be expected to be the result. O if all the power of faith were called out in believing, importunate prayer for the pouring forth of God's blessed Spirit; if Christians, under a deep sense of the utter inefficiency of all means, without divine grace, were to *give themselves* to prayer, and to pray as if it depended on *their* faith and fervor, whether the world should be converted; if all rich men were to give all they could of their wealth, and all other persons were disposed to make sacrifices of luxury and comfort that they might have the more to offer to Christ, if men of intellect, and energy, and influence, were but to consider these resources as belonging to Christ, instead of devoting them to the politics and parties of the world; if all pious females were but to consider the solemn obligations they are under to Christ, not only for his love to their souls, but for the beneficial influence his religion has had upon the condition of their sex; if all the poor were to give of their little, for the spread of the gospel; if, in short, it could be said of all the millions of the disciples of Jesus, each in his sphere, and according to his measure, "*They did what they could*," how far off then would be the answer of the church's prayers, in the universal conversion of the world to Christ? Nothing is wanting but for the church to feel her obligations, to prepare herself for her great work by a fresh baptism of the Spirit, to consecrate her energies to the cause of her divine Lord, and to consider that her great business is the conversion of the world to God, and then the blessing would come.

You, my dear friends, among the rest of Christ's chosen and redeemed people, are called upon to give, in the spirit of faith, and love, and prayer, of your substance to Christ. Sorrowful would be the heart of your pastor, if he saw you wholly taken up in getting wealth for yourselves, and while either hoarding it up to make your children rich, or spending it in the luxuries that constitute "the pride of life," withholding it from the cause of Christ, or niggardly, grudgingly, and scantily yielding it to the urgency of importunate appeals.

Consider, I entreat you, the different results of the property you spend upon yourselves, and that which you spend upon Christ: the former perishes in the using, the latter acquires an imperishable existence. What you lay out in the comforts and elegances of life, yea, and what you lay up unnecessarily, dies with you, when you die, and obtains no resurrection, for it has no principle of immortality. You will see it in no form in another world, for it contains no seed that bears fruit in eternity. It will pass away for ever, and nothing of it remain but the remembrance, and the regret, if, indeed, regret can enter heaven, that it had not been spent for God. But the wealth which, under the influence of pure motives, we devote to Christ, will never die; this is immortal and incorruptible, not, indeed, in the form of property, for of what use would this be to us in heaven? but in what is infinitely more glorious and gratifying, in the form of those redeemed and blessed spirits of just men made perfect, whom it has been employed to convert to God. Yes, the men who give their property for the conversion of souls, may be said, in one sense, to transmute it into those living substances of holiness and bliss, which fill the upper world. This, in the best and fullest sense of the term, is "to lay up treasures in heaven;" it is to enrich the celestial city; to increase the glory of the New Jerusalem; and to place fresh gems in the mediatorial crown of the Redeemer. What a motive to liberality! What an incentive to munificence! How does it soften the labor of getting wealth, sweeten and sanctify the enjoyment of it, and compensate for any little sacrifice we may make in parting from it, to recollect that by giving it to Christ, we impart to it a principle of immortality, and add it to the inheritance, incorruptible, undefiled, and that fadeth not away. Dull must be the heart which such a motive cannot quicken; grovelling the spirit which such a prospect does not elevate. Oh Christians! how is it that we can cheat ourselves of such heavenly felicity and eternal honor, merely to have a little more comfort, luxury, or elegance here? Why do we empoverish ourselves in another world, to enrich ourselves in this? How is it, that the prospect of seeing our property for ever before our eyes, in the forms of glorified spirits; of laying it up around the throne of the Eternal; of adding, by it, to the splendors of the holy of holies; and multiplying the objects on which the eye of Christ shall rest with satisfaction, as the travail of his soul, does not induce us to part with more of it for such purposes, and make us willing to submit to every kind of sacrifice? How is it, I say? Just because of the weakness of our faith. We do not believe these facts, or we believe them with a faith so feeble and so wavering, as scarcely to deserve the name.

How much pleading, and remonstrance, and rebuke, might be spared; how much of the modern system of combating the spirit of worldliness in the disciples of Christ, and producing a spirit of liberality, which, after all, is sluggish, grudging, and reluctant, might be dispensed with; how many of the present devices for getting money, some of them unworthy of the dignity and sanctity of the cause, and nearly all of them a reproach upon its professed supporters, might be abandoned, if Christians understood and believed what they professed; if they lived by faith; if their faith regulated their doings, as well as their sayings; if it regulated their doings for others, as well as for themselves; and if it also regulated their doings in the way of disposing of their property for the salvation of men's souls. The worm at the root of liberality, as well as of every other virtue, is unbelief; and there it may be detected eating out the strength, impairing the beauty, and preventing the fertility of the plant.

But before I close this address, I come back again to the subject of love to Christ. I am not urging an abstract liberality, a mere habit of giving, apart from this holy and evangelical motive. I have directed you to the example of one whose fragrant offering was presented by a hand that was moved to the act, by a heart that burned with love, and glowed with gratitude to Christ; and that example I am anxious you should imitate, not only in its act, but in its principle. I want you to make the love of Christ the mainspring of *your* obedience, as it is of all *true* obedience: and in order to this, the mainspring must *be* in your heart, and the love of Jesus beat strongly there. Ah, here, here is the defect of the great multitude of professors in the present day, the love of Christ does *not* beat strongly there; the love of Christ does *not* constrain them. True, there is much activity and much liberality, and we rejoice in it, for God employs it for good; but how much of this springs from love to Christ, and how much from the compulsion of example, the force of persuasion, the love of activity, and a spirit of individual and congregational vainglory? Does this liberality flow forth silently, gush out spontaneously, welling up, like some abundant spring, by the secret and powerful law of nature, without the aid of mechanical means; or is it not got up, in whatever quantity, with great labor and much pumping? Changing the metaphor, is this zeal kept in vigorous activity by the healthful nutriment of evangelical truth; by the bread which cometh down from heaven; by eating the flesh and drinking the blood of the Son of God? Or is it not kept alive and active by the various stimulants, cordials, and elixirs, which modern ingenuity supplies?

MARY—MARTHA—SARAH, have you, like your devoted sister of Bethany, done what you could? Take an inventory of the means which the Lord has put into your hands for honoring him, and then look over the list of your contributions. What proportion do your annual charities bear to the cost of your furniture, your wardrobe, your ornaments, your luxuries? Jesus did not withhold from you his very precious blood. What are you willing to do for him? What costly alabaster-box have you broken, will you break for him?

Oh God! bestow upon my flock, and upon their minister, thy grace, that when we meet thee in judgment, we may hear this commendatory testimony from thy gracious lips: "They did what they could."

No. VIII.

LIFE OF FAITH.

My Dear Friends: The subject on which I now address you, is of vital importance to your safety as sinners, and to your comfort as Christians; I mean *the Life of Faith.* It is a subject constantly recurring in your conversation and prayers, yet I fear too little understood, still less felt, and, in some cases, mischievously perverted. I shall begin by removing a gross and grievous misconception, which some have taken up on this momentous topic. To live and walk by faith means, with such persons, nothing more than living in an habitual persuasion that they are Christians. This view rests, of course, upon the notion, that faith is a confidence of their own personal interest in Christ. It is common, therefore, for them to speak of a life of faith, as opposed to a life of frames and feelings. Those times in which we have the most spiritual discernment of God's glory, *sensible* communion with him, and feel our love most ardently drawn out to him, are thought by them to have the least exercise of faith. "There is no need," say they, "for faith *then;* at such times we live by sense: but that when all our graces seem dead, and we can see no evidence whence to draw the favorable conclusion, that we are the children of God, then is the time to walk by faith." Their meaning is, "then is the time to believe all is well, and so rest easy, whether we have the evidence that it is so or not." It is not unfrequently, that the language of the prophet is brought forward to support this false view of the subject: "Who is among you that feareth the Lord, that obeyeth the voice of his servant, that walketh in darkness, and hath no light? Let him trust in the name of the Lord, and stay upon his God." Isaiah l. 10. The darkness here, however, does not mean that which is *spiritual*, or a want of discernment of our being a child of God, but providential, or a want of external prosperity, in which season it is our duty, of course, to trust in God.

There cannot be a more pernicious or unscriptural notion; one that is more dangerous to the individual who entertains it, nor more discreditable to religion, than to resolve the life of faith into a going forward with the persuasion that we are justified in the sight of God, and advancing to glory, notwithstanding the coldness and carnality of our hearts, and the absence of all right frames and feelings toward God and eternal things. That some persons live upon frames and feelings, and put this in place of the life of faith is very true. If, instead of keeping the eye of the mind fixed on Christ, it be ever turned inward upon the mind itself, pleased with beholding some supposed exceldencies there; if our consolation is derived from the good we see in ourselves, rather than from the fulness there is in the Savior; if we imagine that the purposes and dispositions of the divine mind toward us, are as variable as our own emotions, or if, while we profess to place all our dependance on Christ, our religious peace and consolation are regulated more by the amount of actual emotion, than by our perception of the work of the Redeemer, this *is* living upon frames and feelings, and is of course opposed to the life of faith.

There are two passages of the apostle in reference to the subject now before us, which deserve attention; the first is this: "I am crucified with Christ; nevertheless I live; yet not I, but Christ liveth in me: and the life that I now live in the flesh, I live by the faith of the Son of God who loved me, and gave himself for me." Gal. ii. 20. The other is this: "We walk by faith, not by sight." 2 Cor. v. 7. Between the life of faith, and the walk of faith, there is no other difference than what lies between a principle and its operations. This is pointed out in another passage, where the apostle says: "If we *live* in the spirit let us also *walk* in the spirit." Gal. v. 25. The *life* of faith refers to the principle; the *walk*, to its acts and exercises. Both taken together mean, *our being habitually influenced in the state of our minds and conduct, not by visible but invisible objects; the objects which are revealed in the word of God; and of the nature and reality of which we have no evidence but this divine testimony.* Faith is a cordial and practical belief of this testimony, and to live and walk by it, must of course mean our being habitually influenced by those objects which that testimony reveals. It is opposed to corporeal sight, to the discoveries of mere reason, and to the ultimate vision of Christ in glory.

The life of faith may be considered in reference to the various objects which the Scripture reveals.

1. To God. "Without faith it is impossible to please God. He that cometh to God, must believe that he is, and that he is the rewarder of all them that diligently seek him." Heb. xi. 6. It is said of Moses: "He endured as seeing him that is invisible." This is the life and walk of faith with respect to God; a realizing sense of his invisible presence: such a persuasion, derived from the word of God, of his existence, and of his natural and moral perfections, as leads us to all that conduct which he requires. Perhaps this acting of faith toward God, could not be more appropriately described, than by the word used in reference to Enoch, and Noah, where it is said they "*walked with God.*" Gen. v. 24; vi. 9. The expression is striking, and signifies such an habitual sense of the presence of God, and such a reference to him as a man has of the friend who is walking at his side. This then is the life of faith, to believe that we are ever surrounded by an all-seeing, holy, and merciful God, and to conduct ourselves toward him accordingly.

2. See it in reference to CHRIST. "I live by the faith of the son of God," said the apostle. Christ is the great object of justifying saving *faith*. Look unto *me*, believe in *me*, come to *me*, is the reiterated, constant invitation and command of Christ as speaking to us in the Gospel. His person, as God-man, Mediator; his offices, as Prophet, Priest, and King; his perfect atonement, justifying righteousness, and prevailing intercession; his spotless example, holy commands, and gracious promises; his government and kingdom, as revealed in the New Testament, are the glorious objects of our contemplation and belief. To live and walk by faith, is to come daily to Jesus in the exercise of fresh dependance, fresh expectations, and fresh devotedness; it is still to renounce all and everything but Christ as the basis of our hope; it is to see more of his glory and grace continually, and to rejoice with more joy in his unsearchable riches, and inexhaustible fulness; it is to confess that as time rolls on, and eternity advances, he is all our righteousness and strength; it is to feel that as knowledge increases, and grace grows, still we have nothing but Christ, as a ground of confidence; it is in all our conflicts, sins, fears, weaknesses, and woes, to repair afresh to him, and just as we came at first, with a full persuasion that we are welcome, and thus ever to derive strength and courage from him;—this is a life of faith in Christ—to be assured and to feel that as the branch has no life apart from the vine, nor the members from the

head, so we have no spiritual life, but as we abide in him.

3. See it in reference to PROVIDENTIAL DISPENSATIONS. Christ has told us once for all, that "all power in heaven and earth is in his hands." Matthew xxviii. 18. The apostle has repeated the declaration: "He is head over all things to his church." Ephes. i. 22. So minute is the superintendence of his care over his people, that "the very hairs of their head are all numbered." Again and again we are assured, that "they that fear the Lord shall not want any good thing." Psalm xxxiv. xxxvii. That "he who spared not his own Son, but freely delivered him up for us all, shall with him also freely give us all things." Rom. viii. 32. "That all things shall work together for good to them that love God, and who are the called according to his purpose." Rom. viii. 28. "That our light afflictions which are but for a moment, work out for us a far more exceeding and eternal weight of glory." 2 Cor. iv. 17. These are the true and comfortable words of Holy Scripture, and the life of faith consists in believing they are true, and in applying them to all the varying events and occurrences and circumstances of our own individual and humble history. Faith believes that in whatever straits and difficulties we may be found God will never abandon us. It says amid seeming destitution, "God is my shepherd, I shall not want." It replies when all things appear against us, "it is well." It believes that love is at the bottom of

all dispensations, however confounding to our wisdom, or disappointing to our hopes. It hushes the murmur, wipes the tear, and suppresses the complaint, by the persuasion that all will end well. It sings, as did good Habakkuk: "Although the fig-tree shall not blossom, neither shall fruit be in the vines; the labor of the olive shall fail, and the fields shall yield no meat; the flock shall be cut off from the fold, and there shall be no herd in the stalls: yet I will rejoice in the Lord, I will joy in the God of my salvation." Hab. iii. 17, 18.

4. See the life of faith in reference to THE SECOND COMING OF CHRIST. "Ye turned to God from dumb idols, to serve the living and true God, and to wait for his son from heaven." 1 Thess. i. 9, 10. Such was the apostle's description of the habitual frame of the mind of believers in his day. A similar representation we find in another place: "Looking for that blessed hope, and the glorious appearing of the great God, and our Savior Jesus Christ." Titus ii. 13. As if it were the one great object of their expectation, to wait for the second advent of the Savior. If the Millenarians run into one extreme in the prominence they give to this great event in their meditations and discourses, so as to make it predominate even over the *first* coming of Christ, the great bulk of professing Christians run into the opposite extreme of leaving it out too much. Oh, what are all the future events of time; what are the changes that are to take place in the history of our country, or the world, compared

with the advent of Christ, when he shall come a second time without a sin-offering unto salvation? What should be so interesting to our hopes as "the revelation of the Lord Jesus Christ from heaven, with his mighty angels, when he shall come to be glorified in his saints, and admired in all them that believe." 2 Thess. i. 7–10. Illustrious day! Glorious scene! Here is the life of faith, in contemplating these, and giving rise to the most lively and animated hopes; and setting the Christian in the attitude of expectation, and the work of preparation.

5. Contemplate the life of faith in reference TO ETERNITY, and THE GLORY OF HEAVEN. How concisely, yet how beautifully is this expressed by the apostle: "We look not at the things which are seen, but at the things which are not seen; for the things which are seen are temporal, but the things which are not seen are eternal." 2 Cor. iv. 18. Oh, what simplicity, and yet what sublimity of language! It was as if he had said: "Eternity is so clearly revealed to us in all its wonders and glories, and is so vast and magnificent a scene, and withal so near, that we scarcely seem to see the things of time, and have no inclination to turn away from the boundless prospect of immortality to look after them: and in all our estimates, our feelings, and our pursuits, we are guided and controlled by a regard to things eternal." This is the acting of faith, to believe in glory, honor, and immortality; and the life of faith is to let eternity

give the stamp and form of our character. It is to treat heaven as a reality, and to let it mould our very spirit. If this divine principle be in our souls, we shall enter into the apostle's beautiful language and say: "We know that if our earthly house of this tabernacle were dissolved, we have a building of God, a house not made with hands, eternal in the heavens: for we that are in this tabernacle do groan, being burdened: not for that we would be unclothed, but clothed upon, that mortality might be swallowed up of life. Therefore we are always confident, knowing that while we are at home in the body we are absent from the Lord. For we walk by faith, not by sight." 2 Cor. v. 1–7.

This, my dear friends, is the new, and spiritual, and heavenly life you are called by your profession to lead: this is in fact *the Christian* life. It is to this the apostle refers when he says: "Ye are dead and your life is hid with Christ in God; and when Christ, who is our life, shall appear, then shall ye also appear with him in glory." Col. iii. 3, 4. How different to all this is the way of the multitude, "who are walking according to the course of this world."—"They mind earthly things." Their whole frame and temper of mind is expressed in the inquiry: "Who will *show* us any good?" Sense is their region, and they never rise out of it. Their only converse is with the visible world. Beyond this they have no objects, either of hope or fear; no springs of happiness;

no sources of interest. And even among those who make a profession of religion, how little is this subject understood and felt. How low is this heavenly life, how feeble is the pulse of faith. Do not the great bulk of those who call themselves Christians appear to be living far too much by sense? Not indeed that they are immersed in vice or gayety; but how deeply sunk in worldly care, how taken up with worldly comforts! No matter how pure, and how innocent the things may be in themselves, if they hide scriptural objects from the eye of faith, they are unlawful, as to their influence, when they do this. Our profession implies a disposition, and a habit of seeking our highest objects of interest and delight in things unseen and eternal; a daily converse of the soul with God and Christ; with heaven and eternity. He that is thus walking will not allow himself to be long out of sight of the cross; will not wander far from God in quest of happiness. He will not shut himself up amid terrestrial scenes, however rational or innocent. He has a new principle in his nature, beside sense and reason, for he has faith; and this is a restless, powerful, and craving one, which aspires after something higher, and better, and more enduring, than anything he can see, or touch, or taste. He is the subject of wants and woes, which only faith can relieve and mitigate. Neither sense nor reason can assist him to throw off his load of guilt, or give satisfaction to desires which the world is too poor to gratify. Here, therefore, on this globe, he finds himself a prisoner, sighing for escape from the dark and limited region which he inhabits: and it is only faith that can open for him the doors, and make way for his excursion into the invisible realities of eternity.

Alas! how small are our attainments in this divine life, how much are we occupied and engrossed by things of time and sense. It is well worth while to ask, what you know of this? You are all living by faith or sight; either upon things heavenly, or things earthly. On what is *your* soul living? What is it that supplies *your* comfort? Where does *your* spirit go daily to quench her thirst after happiness; to the breaking cisterns of created good, or to the fountains of living waters? Sooner or later, the fullest store of the joys of sense will be exhausted. "All the dear delights of earth are but the brood of time, a brood that will soon take to themselves wings, and, with him that that cherished them, fly away. Oh my friends, it is but too common for many to suppose that those who live by faith in the enjoyments of the world to come, live upon mere imaginations. But are they not mistaken? It is *their* enjoyments, and not those of believers that are imaginary. Pleasures, profits, honors, what are *they?* The whole form only a kind of *ideal* world, a sort of splendid *show*, like that in a dream, which when you awake, all is gone. To grasp it, is to grasp a shadow; and to feed upon it, is to feed upon the wind." Christ and his salvation—heaven and eternity—are the only substantial realities; and these are the objects for which faith lives, and toward which it is perpetually walking.

Receive then, dear friends, the word of exhortation, and seek to possess more and more of this divine life. Understand clearly the nature and operation of that great principle, which is the root of all true piety. It is not only as sinners, and for the purpose of justification, that you need faith, but as Christians also for sanctification, consolation, and perseverance. Every act of the spiritual life is an act of faith; every step in the spiritual walk is a step of faith. The Christian's course is not one of *doing* merely, but of *believing*. His prayers are the breathings of faith; his works are the actings of faith; his penitence is the tear of faith; his joy is the smile of faith; his hopes are the anticipations of faith; his fears are the tremblings of faith; his strength is the confidence of faith; his submission is the acquiescence of faith. It is the eye that looks at Christ; the foot that moves to him; the hand that receives him; the mouth that feeds upon him. It is not only by the activity of obedience, but by the silent and passive power of dependance, that the Christian is strong and victorious. Here is the reason why so many professors are so worldly and so weak; why they make such little progress, and such small attainments; some of them are so much under the dominion of sense, are so almost wholly given up to a life of sight that they have neither time nor inclination to look at the things that are unseen and eternal: while others, though far more solicitous and laborious about spiritual things, fix their attention, and exhaust their energies, upon toilsome self-sustained struggles, to the neglect of faith. There is in them no habitual looking to Christ, no abiding in him, no vivid consciousness that all their springs are in him, and that it is from his fulness they are to receive and grace for grace. Theirs is a life of working, but not of believing; they are lamentably ignorant of the astonishing mightiness, yea, the all-mightiness, there is in the simple act of believing; for what is this, but to be strong in the Lord, and in the power of his might?

Do not forget that it is not possible to carry on the growth of the Christian life unto the measure of the stature of the fulness of Christ, apart from this. "It is only when that life is firmly-rooted and grounded in faith, that the straight stem of righteousness will rise up, and branch out into the manifold ramifications of duty, and that it will be crowned with the brightness and sweetness of the amaranthine blossoms of love. When moral rectitude is disjoined from faith, there is no trust in it. It may stiffen into pharisaical formality, or ossify into stoical severity; or it may be withered by the blights and cankerworm of expediency; or it may tumble into the stye of Epicureanism and rot there. When love is disjoined from faith there is no trust in it. Caprice may throw it to the winds; chance may nip it in the bud; pride may blast it; vanity may eat away its core; prosperity may parch it; distress may freeze it: lust may taint and poison it; the slights and neglects which it must needs experience at times, in a world of frailty and mutability, will assuredly sour and embitter it. Indeed, according to the true idea of Christian love, and of righteousness, neither the one nor the other can exist at all, except as springing out of faith. Whereas, when faith is genuine and strong, in proportion to its genuineness and strength, will it infallibly produce righteousness and love; a righteousness and love which, having a living seed within them, will be abiding." A living faith, and living works must, and do, always go together: they cannot live but in union with each other, cut them asunder, and they both die. To think of growing in grace, increasing in love, and abounding in the fruits of righteousness, which are by Jesus Christ unto the glory of God, in any other way than by faith, and strong faith too, is as irrational as to cut off the branch from the vine, and to expect it, in that state, to bear the rich, full clusters of the parent-tree.

It is by "the Life of Faith," you will bring glory to God. Confidence in the kindness, veracity, and ability of a fellow-creature, affords a pleasure to his own mind, and does him honor before others. We please God, and magnify him before the world, when we confide in him. For this purpose we are placed *where* we are, and *as* we are, where we can see nothing, hear nothing, touch nothing, but must believe everything: and all this that we might glorify him as a God that is faithful and cannot lie. We see not God, nor Christ, nor heaven, and know nothing about them, but by the testimony of Scripture. How then is God honored, when upon the credit of his simple word alone, we prefer the invisible realities of eternity, to the visible things of time; and amid all that is dazzling to sense, gratifying to appetite, and dear to passion, spend a life of self-denial, mortification, and separation from the world; and in some instances die the martyr's death.

Prove youselves, then, the children of faithful Abraham, and stagger not at the promises of God, through unbelief; but be *strong in faith*, GIVING GLORY TO GOD. Believer, if you are brought into dark and difficult circumstances, instead of allowing yourself to think you may stand excused for the indulgence of murmuring and unbelief, consider it rather as an opportunity and a call for the exercise of faith, and for thus glorifying God. The thicker the darkness through which he calls you to pass, and the more entirely destitute you are of all help from every other quarter, the greater is the opportunity for honoring him by trusting him with all your concerns.

How blessed to its possessor is the life of faith. "Believing in Christ, we rejoice with joy unspeakable and full of glory."—"Because thou hast seen me," said Christ to Thomas, "thou hast believed;

blessed are they that have not seen, and yet have believed." John xx. How sweetly does confidence even in an earthly friend, relieve the mind from distressing fears and apprehensions; and this relief is in exact proportion to the ability and willingness of this friend to assist us, and the benefits we expect from his generosity. What then must be the relief afforded to the agitated mind of the Christian, by confidence in God, reliance on Christ, and the hope of glory. "Great and wonderful is the consolation such a life affords. In all the vicissitudes of life and horrors of death, nothing can cheer and fortify the mind like this. By faith in Christ, and the unseen world, we can endure injuries without revenge, afflictions without fainting, and losses without despair. Let the nations of the earth clash like potsherds, one against another; yea, let nature herself approach toward her final dissolution; let her groan as being ready to expire, and sink into her primitive nothing: still the believer lives! His all is not on board that vessel! His chief inheritance lies in another soil."

> "His hand the good man fastens on the skies,
> And bids earth roll, nor feels her idle whirl."

How obvious is this to the most superficial thinker! Faith, when the report believed is a joyful one, must be productive of delight. Who can believe glad tidings and not be made glad? Hence the reasonableness of those exhortations which call upon us to rejoice in the Lord. There is more real happiness in the believer's mind, when in the very midst of poverty and trouble he exercises a lively confidence in God, than the richest worldling on earth enjoys, when surrounded by all his untold wealth, and incalculable possessions. To feel our own poverty, emptiness, nothingness, and yet at the same time to feel in all the confidence of faith, our fulness in Christ and our title to an inheritance, incorruptible, undefiled, and that fadeth not away, is one of the most felicitous states of mind we can attain to in this world, uniting as it does, the deepest humility with the most exalted and triumphant anticipations.

The life of faith will not last always, but will give way to a life of eternal vision. We are walking by faith to see Jesus as he is, and to be like him. "Thy word," said the Psalmist, "is a light unto my feet, a lamp unto my path:" and faith is the hand that holds it, as we pass through the darkness of this our earthly sojourn, and the deeper shadows of the grave: but when our spirits emerge into the regions of glory and the realms of immortality, we shall need the lamp no longer, for "there is no night there." Oh, what a moment will that be when the lamp of faith will be suddenly extinguished, not amid the darkness of eternal night, but amid the splendors of everlasting day and the prospects of the heavenly world, and its tiny spark shall be lost amid the blaze of glory pouring from the throne of God! How will the soul endure the scene which shall then burst upon her view?

Be this then your prayer, my dear friends, your sincere and earnest prayer: "Lord, increase our faith." Be willing to have the world displaced from your soul, to make room for the objects of faith; and be ever ready to come from the dazzling glare of earthly scenes, to feel the steady illumination, and dwell in the calm and holy light that shines from heaven on your path. Study as well as read the Scriptures, and meditate much upon their contents. Frequent and devout converse with the objects of faith, is the best way to have it increased. Watch diligently against the influence of those objects which have a fatal tendency to eclipse its light, to obstruct its operation, and enfeeble its life; namely, sensual pleasure; eager pursuit of the world; and a too intimate converse with those who mind earthly things.

No. IX.

INFLUENCE OF OLDER CHRISTIANS.

My Dear Friends: A subject of considerable interest and importance has often occurred to me, when meditating on the state of the Christian Church, and that is, *the influence which the conduct of its senior members has over those who have lately commenced the divine life.* It is obvious from all the principles of our nature, that this must be considerable, either for good or for evil; and that if it do not encourage and strengthen them in the way, it must enfeeble and dishearten them. It is so fearful a thing to cast stumbling-blocks in the path of a Christian brother, and to disturb his peace, much more to endanger his soul, that it becomes us all to take heed to our steps, both for his sake and our own.

You must be aware that those who are but lately converted to God, and have just assumed the Christian profession, look with attention and deference to others of long-standing in the church, and are apt to make them their patterns and standards. In the army, the veteran soldiers have great influence in training the young recruits, in forming their character, and fitting them for service: in a manufactory, the habits of the workmen have a considerable share in guiding those of the apprentices; and in a family, the younger children imitate the older ones. Thus it is in the church of God, the younger look up to those who are more advanced in age, or in experience. It is very true that they have a perfect standard in the word of God, which they ought to consult, and to which they ought to seek for grace to conform themselves, without considering what other and older believers do. Instead, however, of studying the nature, and claims, and extent of vital Christianity in its own inspired records, and thus imitating the divine original, they are but too apt to look at it as it is to be seen in their fellow-professors, and thus by copying *from* a copy, and that but an imperfect one too, they go on multiplying the sadly defective exhibitions of practical religion, with which the church always abounds. It is not, however, till they have experienced considerable surprise by their first acquaintance with these imperfect patterns, that they are brought to imitate them.

"It has not, I believe, unfrequently occurred that young converts in the ardor of their first love, and while much unacquainted as yet, with what is called the religious world, have looked upon the church of Christ, as a sacred enclosure, within which dwelt scarcely any other than a kind of heavenly inhabitants, as a sort of vestibule to the temple above, where as these blessed spirits were putting off their earthly affections, and preparing to enter into the presence of their divine Redeemer, they could think or speak of little else than the glory that awaited them; and by whom every addition to their number would be hailed with delight, and welcomed as an accession to the fervor of their piety. In such society, these novices expected soon to attain to the full maturity of the Christian character, and ripen into the greatest perfection attainable on earth. They anticipated the sweetest and holiest intercourse, an almost unearthly spirituality, and an uninterrupted strain of religious conversation in the communion of saints--but alas! what a woful disappointment did the reality produce; in the sacred enclosure they found worldly-minded professors, almost as intent upon things seen and temporal, as any they had left without the gates; in the vestibule of heaven, they beheld men and women covered with the dust, disordered with the anxieties, and given up to the enjoyment of earth. They saw little but the world in conduct, and heard little else in conversation. A cold chill fell upon their hearts, which seemed at once, like a frosty atmosphere acting upon a newly-exposed plant, to check the ardor of their religious affections; and even they, lately so fervent, soon sunk and settled down into the lukewarmness of those among whom they had come to dwell. It is true they expected too much; they had formed a standard for the church militant, too nearly approaching that of the church triumphant; but still, even persons with a more correct knowledge of professing Christians, and with more sober expectations of what was to be derived from them, have upon coming among them, experienced much less of the benefits of fellowship than they expected. This should not be. Happily it is not always thus. In our churches are to be found some, who by their knowledge, piety, and experience, are nursing fathers and mothers of the young Christian, and who, by the blessing of God, breathe into him their own spirit."

In this way it is that the church of God is kept down in its spiritual attainments, and does not make that advance to the higher degrees of knowledge, faith, and holiness, which might be expected, and which is so much to be desired. I have no need to prove that the church is not distinguished in our day by the eminence of its spirituality and heavenly-mindedness. It has much zeal, activity, and liberality, and in these things we cordially rejoice, but they are most fearfully mixed up with a prevailing worldliness in many of its aspects and operations; and it may be feared that the dazzling splendor of missionary movements, and the bustling scenes of zealous labor, have too much drawn away Christians from deep communion with their own hearts, and with the spirit of God. What a flexible and accommodating morality has infected our business transactions! What an acrimonious and uncharitable spirit has soured the temper of the various denominations toward each other! What a languid faith, and feeble fluttering hope, characterize the frame of the bulk of professors! As if the missionary ardor might be accepted as a compromise for all deficiencies in the more laborious, painful, and self-denying exertions of the Christian life. External action and doing, has with many, become a substitute, for heart-watchfulness, the subduing of sin, and holy communion with the spirit. And to whom are these deficiencies to be attributed but to the older professors of religion? Were *they* generally as eminent as they should be; were they patterns of that elevated, consistent, experimental religion, which might justly be looked for from the growth of twenty, thirty, or forty years; were they free from the inconsistencies, which mar the beauty, and diminish the power of the Christian profession; were they shining as lights in the world, reflecting the beauties of holiness, breathing the spirit of devotion, and abounding in the fruits of righteousness, which are by Jesus Christ unto the glory of God; then the younger brethren and sisters, as they were born into the family of God, would be likely to partake of their spirit, to follow their conduct, and imitate their character; and a succession of eminent and devoted professors would be maintained.

I do not mean to say, or to insinuate, that the senior members of the church under my care are more deficient than those of other churches. Certainly not. There are not a few of you who are "my joy and hope," and will be, I trust, "my crown of rejoicing in the presence of our Lord, at his coming." I write for others who are not the subjects of my pastoral oversight, as well as for you, and am laying down general principles, for universal application.

May I then, my dear friends, solicit your serious and prayerful attention to the subject of this Address; you I refer to, who have, in age and standing, already attained to the character of fathers and mothers in Israel, or who are advancing to it. Do not dismiss the matter as of no importance, nor let your modesty or your indifference lead you to imagine that your influence is less than I have stated, and that therefore the subject is not worth your consideration. Do not refuse to examine, and well weigh it. You *are* doing good or harm, to younger Christians. They *will* consider your conduct, whether you wish it or no. Their eyes are open to what you do, and their ears to what you say, when you little think of it. You cannot retire from observation, nor dwell in seclusion so deep as to elude all scrutiny. You *must* be influential. You ought not to wish, or attempt to be negative. You are a candle lighted, to be put, not under a bushel, but in a candlestick, to give light to all that are in the house. Younger professors are continually coming around you, both in the transactions of business, and in the intercourse of friendship, and are imbibing an influence from you, whether you intentionally exert it or not. Their character is forming imperceptibly by you, unconsciously to themselves, under the power of your example. There is no need of your saying, "Act as I do;" nor of their replying, "I will." The influence goes on without such formalities. Their tone of piety rises or falls to the key-note you strike: their zeal cools or grows warm by yours: moral principles fasten or loosen their roots in their hearts, as yours appear to be fixed or fluctuating.

I am aware that this influence has limitations, and that many new converts to God, set out on the life and walk of faith, with such a decision of character, such a strong faith, and such an ardent love, as to resist the example, and condemn the worldly-mindedness of many of those who have been long in the way of godliness. They retain their spirituality and devotional feeling amid much that is calculated to repress them: but to do so, they find it necessary to retire from the intimacy of many who had been in Christ long before them.

If *you* are not aware of the importance of this subject, the pastors of the churches are. They know, and some of them bitterly lament, the influence of their elder members. They see amid all their zeal and solicitude to raise the tone of piety in their churches, a counteracting power exerted by many who ought to be foremost in lending their help to forward so desirable an object. I know both clergymen of the Church of England, as well as Dissenting Ministers, to whom this must be a sore grievance. The pastors will labor to a considerable extent in vain, in endeavoring publicly to promote the spirituality of their flocks, if the more influential members of the community do not sustain their efforts in private.

Be careful, then, not to throw stumbling-blocks in a brother's way, even in little things. There are two ways in which you may do this: First, *by doing what is positively wrong, or of doubtful propriety.* I do not now allude to immoralities and vice. Such things, I am happy to say, rarely, very rarely, occur among us, but I refer to the lesser violations of Christian propriety; such for instance, as the indulgence of bad tempers; offences against love, gratitude, and humility; the practice of those dishonorable artifices which are so common in the modern system of trade; conformity to the world in spirit, entertainments, dress, and amusements; and covetousness, hard-heartedness, and indifference to the cause of religion in the world. Fathers and mothers in Israel, I beseech you, for the sake of the "young men," and the "little children," that you abstain from such things. Do not give the sanction of your example, the aid of your influence, to the spread of a diseased religious profession, in which such leprous spots as these are continually breaking out.

And should there happen to be anything of *doubtful propriety*, a mere matter of taste and gratification; a matter about which the Christian world are somewhat divided; a matter condemned by the more spiritual part of the church; a matter seemingly though not in reality, at best half way between good and evil, resting on the very line of demarcation between right and wrong, partly on one territory and partly on the other; in such a case, the better instructed and more experienced members, should abstain from these appearances of evil. Should not they be the first to set the example, and to give out a pattern of self-denial? Should not they be the leaders of the cross-bearing company? Should not their younger brethren and sisters see how far advanced they are in the virtues of forbearance, temperance, and separation from the world? Should not they lend their aid in training the new converts to that hardy, enduring, self-denying religion, which is implied in the Christian profession? Observe the example of the apostle PAUL. Speaking of eating meats offered to idols, he says: "Take heed lest by any means this liberty of yours becomes a stumbling-block to them that are weak. And through thy knowledge shall thy weak brother perish, for whom Christ died? But when ye sin so against the brethren, and wound their weak conscience, ye sin against Christ. Wherefore, if meat make my brother to offend, I will eat no flesh while the world standeth, lest I make my brother to offend." 1 Cor. viii. The general sentiment contained in this beautiful and generous passage, is an affectionate solicitude on the part of older, and better instructed, and stronger professors, not to enjoy any gratification, or to do anything, which should have the tendency to pervert the principles, mislead the conscience, perplex the reasonings, or grieve the minds of such as are weaker or younger in the faith. What arguments and motives does the passage contain! By misleading such persons we sin against the brethren, wound weak consciences, endanger immortal souls, sin against Christ! Aged professors read this; ponder it; tremble; and decide.

It is also to be remembered that it is not merely the *whole course* of a Christian's conduct that has this influence, but perhaps some one single transaction, different from the one I have just supposed, which is regarded as a sort of test-act by younger converts. There is some *one* decision which he is to make, some single instance which he is to exhibit, some isolated position which he is to occupy, upon the manner of conducting himself in which, many will form an opinion, not simply of *his* character, but of the rule which they are to prescribe to themselves. His conduct in that one transaction, will perhaps, send out an extensive and permanent influence over the whole character of many. If he has grace to act well in that instance, *they* will be led at once, in imitation of his example, to adopt a high standard, a lofty model of Christian profession; they will depart with a high notion of what is required in a follower of Christ, and with a fixed and determined purpose to follow whatsoever things are lovely and of good report. Whereas, if unhappily *he* fail, and exhibit a flexibility of principle, and a spirit of compromise, *they*, from that hour, obtain in his conduct, an apology to others, and a quietus to their conscience, for an unspiritual, worldly-minded, and inconsistent profession.

SECONDLY. You may put stumbling-blocks in the way of younger Christians, not only by doing what is wrong, but by *not doing what is right;* by a deficiency for instance, in seriousness, devoutness, diligence, and spirituality. There is a radical defect in the religion of many professors, not in morality, but in spirituality. They do not appear *in earnest.* Their character and conduct do not bear and exhibit with sufficient distinctness, the impress of the cross; the image of God; the seal of the spirit; the stamp of eternity; the likeness of heaven. A Christian is, or should be, a man who takes not only the form, but the *hue* of his character from the Bible; and that should be a hue of heavenly color. Now where this to a considerable extent is wanting in older professors, its influence on younger ones must be sad indeed. If they hear little of devout conversation from your lips, they cannot of course attach any great value to spirituality of mind. If they see you habitually absent from the prayer-meetings, they cannot entertain any ideas of the importance of social prayer. If they do not see you at the week-day sermon, they are not likely to feel it of any consequence to take an hour from business or pleasure, to be there themselves. If they hear you murmuring and discontented, impatient and rebellious; or even if they see you gloomy, cheerless, and disconsolate in trouble and sickness, how it must tend to diminish their sense of the power and value of religion, and to discourage them in the prospect of affliction, which may be coming upon them. O my beloved friends, do consider these things: and the Lord give you understanding.

These remarks apply, of course, with peculiar force to such of you as are parents, and are masters and mistresses, and who have fellow-members in your own household, among your children and servants. What patterns of godliness should such young Christians expect to see in us! And what expectations of this kind have they not a right to entertain? Have we any reason to be astonished, or to complain of their *low* degrees of piety, if ours are not *high?* Let me remind you that it is not the unconverted branches of our families, that should excite our solicitude, and engage our care, but the professedly converted. While we should be anxious to bring the former under the influence of religion, we should also be no less so, to carry on the others to higher degrees of religion. Let us ask if our conduct at home is of such a nature, as is calculated to make the piety of home flourish around us. Is there that consistency, that spirituality, that amiableness, that regularity in private prayer, and that fervor at the family altar, which shall encourage, instruct, confirm, and assist the young disciples which sit or wait at our table?

How emphatically does this subject speak to the Deacons of our Churches! They, as office-bearers, are, next to the pastor, the most prominent members of the community of saints. "What manner of persons ought *they* to be in all holy conversation and godliness." They, like the Pastor, should be "ensamples to the flock." In the original directions given by the apostle to the mother-church at Jerusalem, for the choice of these officers, its members were to look out for "men of honest report, *full of the Holy Ghost*, and wisdom." And they chose STEPHEN, and others, "*full of faith and the Holy Ghost.*" Acts vi. How solemn, how holy, how responsible, and in some respects, how fearful a thing is it to bear office in the church of Christ; in that church which he has purchased with his blood, which he died on the cross to redeem, and lives to govern as a priest upon his throne. What men should our *Deacons* be, as well as our pastors! How holy, how spiritual, how sympathizing, how diligent, how devoted to the welfare of the church! As they hold their walks amid the members on sacramental seasons, distributing the memorials of the Savior's dying love, with what reverence and affection should they be beheld, as men of unblemished reputation, and of eminent piety! What sacrifices of time, taste, and gratification; what self-denial, and labor; should they not be prepared to make for the benefit of the members? Wisdom in council, skill in managing the secular affairs of the church, tact in business, are not the only qualifications required in them, who are placed so near the ark, but the spirit of faith, prayer, and eminent piety. As they stand and wait in the house, or minister at the table of the Lord, it should be as clad in the livery of holiness, and bearing the image of Christ. Whoever is deficient in piety, it should not be they. Whoever casts stumbling-blocks in the way of the brethren, it should not be they. If the spirit of godliness were about to depart from the church, they should stand in the gap, and prevent the glory from leaving the temple.

This subject however does not appertain exclusively to any one class of our senior members, but belongs to them all. The apostle takes it for granted that a Christian's attainments and usefulness should be in proportion to the date of his profession: "When for the *time* ye ought to be teachers," was his language to the believing Hebrews. What then ought to be the extent of *your* knowledge, the maturity of your graces, the depth of your experience, the perfection of your example, the power of your influence, and the measure of your usefulness, who have been planted so many years in the courts of the Lord? What a beautiful record is it in sacred history of Aquila and Priscilla, that this holy pair employed their riper knowledge and their richer grace in instructing the young and eloquent Apollos in the way of the Lord more perfectly. And you know a preacher and a pastor, who is not ashamed to avow his obligations to a poor and godly couple, long since gone to their rest, who by their simple piety, consistent conduct, friendly disposition and mature experience, nurtured the germe of religion in his heart, and helped to train the young disciple for usefulness in the church of God. They watched him with the solicitude of a father and mother in Israel, instructed him in their lowly cot, in the principles of the gospel, relieved his perplexities, gathered out the stones from his path, and aided to establish him in the paths of righteousness and peace. How few of the older disciples of the Lord, are thus disposed to open their doors to the young inquirers after truth and salvation, and to act the part of nursing fathers and nursing mothers, to the new-born babes in Christ. How useful might be THE OLDER FEMALE MEMBERS of the churches, in employing those seasons of intercourse which are continually occurring with their younger friends, to cherish in their minds the spirit of faith, prayer, and holiness. Instead of this, is not too much of the time spent in useless gossip, frivolous chit-chat, and vain discourse on fashion, dress, and news? O ye matronly professors, consider how important is the right formation of the female character. Recollect that those young women, who frequent your house, listen to your conversation, and are looking up to you as examples, will perhaps, be one day placed at the heads of the families like you, and will exert some influence upon the world, through their husbands and their children: and recollect also, that they will be likely to take the tone of their religion, the standard of their womanly piety from you. Endeavor, then, to breathe into their souls the spirit of ardent and consistent religion, repress the disposition to vanity, mould them to sobriety of judgment, and train them, as you have opportunity, to elevated sentiments of usefulness. Blessed is that woman, she is *indeed* a mother in Israel, who, by her amiable, cheerful disposition, united with good sense and engaging manners, attracts the younger females to her society; and who, when they are gathered round her, exerts her influence to render them blessings, both to the church and to the world. It is an ill sign for a middle-aged female professor of religion, when the more frivolous of the young are the fondest of her society, and the more spiritual retire from it. Perhaps some will reply: "We ought to exhibit religion to young people with a cheerful aspect." Certainly you ought. I wish you to appear ever happy in their presence; the very type of peace; carrying, in the sunshine of your countenances, the index of a mind at rest, and a proof that you are the children of light, *walking* in light;—but this is different from froth, and merriment, and levity. The cheerfulness of a Christian should be joy and peace *in believing;* rejoicing *in the Lord*, a serious joy, a joyful seriousness. "Speak thou the words which become sound doctrine, that the aged women be in behavior as becometh holiness—teachers of good things; that they may teach the young women to be sober, to love their husbands, to ove their children, to be discreet, chaste, keepers at home—that the word of God be not blasphemed." Titus ii.

Let all, then, whether male or female, solemnly inquire, whether they have ever yet sufficiently estimated the importance of the subject of this address. Let them recollect what their own ideas and expectations were of older Christians, when they entered the church, and what surprise and disappointment they experienced. Let them consider in what light it may be supposed they now appear, to those younger believers who have lately become acquainted with them, and ask themselves if no surprise has been felt at seeing them no more distinguished for spiritual attainment. Let them look round, and see if some are not violating consistency, and pleading their example. Let them especially remember, how responsible is their situation, and how fearful a thing it is to be the means of lowering in young believers, the ideas of the solemnity and spirituality of the Christian profession, and of spreading lukewarmness through the Christian church.

Young believers, I would conclude with a few hints to *you*. Do not expect to find the Church of Christ composed of spotless characters. Do not allow yourselves to be staggered, almost to halting, by the imperfections you observe in older professors. You will see in the interior of the church some things that will perplex you. Still, however, remember that if there be more sin among professors than you expected, there is also more holiness than you see or know. Multitudes of eminent Christians are unknown to you, and it is perhaps the most inconsistent ones that you happen to know best. Guard against a censorious, suspicious, and arraigning temper. Cultivate the spirit of charity, so beautifully described in 1 Cor. xiii. and be as candid toward the imperfections of others, as a regard to the claims of truth and holiness will allow; and no more. Especially remember to guard against the insidious influence of the defects and inconsistencies of older professors. Adopt as your standard the word of God. Take up your opinion of what religion is, by looking at this, not at the conduct of senior Christians, or any Christians. He that would form a correct idea of the glory of the sun, must see the luminary as he shines from a cloudless sky, and not as he is reflected, in a distorted form, from the troubled surface of the turbid lake.

No. X.

THE SPIRIT OF PRAYER.

My Dear Friends: Very little need be said to prove to you that the duty and privilege of prayer appertain to a believer in Christ, and occupy a high place among the obligations and delights of the child of God. The whole Bible teaches us the importance, necessity, and blessedness of this devout exercise of the soul. The Old Testament, as well as the New, proves that the spirit of true godliness is a spirit of supplication; and the Psalms of David will ever remain a manual of devotion for the believer, in which he will ever find some of the fittest words to pour out the breathings of his heart to God. What I design in this address, then, is not so much to state the obligations to prayer, as to enforce the cultivation of the spirit of prayer.

In almost all occupations, acts, and habits, in which man can be engaged, and which recur at regularly returning periods, there are both spirit and form; in other words, the visible action, and the animating spirit imbodied in that action; hence we speak of the *spirit* of patriotism, of commerce, of enterprise, of religion, of prayer—by which we mean a something beside the action and of which the action is but the expression. The idea is taken from the compound nature of man, where, beside the outward and visible form, there is the inward and invisible soul, by which the former lives, moves, and acts. Now as there may be the form of man without the spirit of man, so there may be the form of any particular virtue or exercise, without the living animating spirit. The apostle speaks of some who have the "form of godliness, but deny the power [*i. e.*, the spirit] thereof:" 2 Tim. iii. 5. And what is said of godliness as a whole, may be said of that particular part of it which I am now considering.

I shall therefore state what I mean by "the spirit of prayer," and then enjoin its cultivation.

To the possession of this spirit it is necessary we should have *a large measure of those elements of which all true prayer is composed.* There must be *a deep, abiding, and impressive sense of want;* for prayer is the language of felt necessity. Our sense of guilt, depravity, ignorance, weakness, folly, danger, must be lively, penetrating, and humbling. Without this sense of want, praying is only words and heartless forms; mere hypocritical pretence; a mimicry of devotion; while on the other hand, the more we have of this, the more we have of the spirit of prayer. Is this then our view of our state? Do we carry about with us continually an affecting consciousness of our numerous and pressing wants? Have we a sense of destitution, always humbling, often afflictive and oppressive?

Do we "groan, being burdened," under a sense of our guilt and weakness? The feeling of fulness and sufficiency, whether of strength or anything else, is the very opposite of the spirit of prayer. The church of Laodicea, which said "they were rich and increased with goods, and had need of nothing," could have had none of the element of prayer. Poverty of spirit is essential to this.

But connected with this, and arising out of it, there must be *a conscious dependance upon God:* a habit of regarding him, and looking to him as the source of supply: a feeling similar to what the Psalmist experienced when he said: "All my springs are in thee."—"My soul wait thou only upon God, for my expectation is from him."—"I will lift up my eyes unto the hills, whence cometh my help. My help cometh from the Lord who made heaven and earth."—"With thee is the fountain of life." A prevailing habit of dependance upon God, a consciousness that he is our only and all-sufficient resource, is the very spirit of prayer.

To this must be added *the exercise of faith and confidence in God through Christ.* "He that cometh to God must believe that he is, and that he is the rewarder of all them that diligently seek him." Without faith there can be no acceptable worship. "Let him ask in faith, nothing wavering," said the apostle, "for he that wavereth is like a wave of the sea driven with the wind and tossed. For let not that man think he shall receive anything of the Lord." James i. 6, 7. We must believe in God's character as a God of love, delighting to dispense happiness to his creatures; as a God of wisdom and power, able and willing to do exceeding abundantly above all we can ask or think. We must believe that prayer is his own appointed method of approaching him, and that which is agreeable to him, welcome to him, and well-pleasing in his eyes; that we can never please him better than when we go with enlarged desires after spiritual blessings to his throne; nor do him greater honor than when we expect large communications of his grace. We must believe in Christ as the only way to the Father, and believe that by *this* way, and this only, he is ever accessible. Such a faith is a necessary and an important element in the spirit of prayer. The stronger and more prevailing this is, the more fervent and delightful will be our supplications at the throne of the heavenly majesty. By such views of God and Christ, we shall be irresistibly drawn to the footstool of divine mercy. Our lukewarmness will kindle into holy warmth under such persuasions of the inexhaustible bounty of God, and we shall feel the sweet attractions of his love, dissipating our fears, removing our reluctance, and engaging our confidence.

The spirit of adoption as a fruit of this faith, is also an element of the spirit of prayer. We are to come with *boldness* to the throne of grace. That is, we are to come in the spirit of a child, conscious that he is ever welcome to his Father in heaven.

This is beautifully described by the apostle where he says: "Ye have not received the spirit of bondage again to fear; but ye have received the spirit of adoption, whereby we cry, Abba, Father." Rom. viii. 15. None can pray acceptably to God or comfortably to themselves, but in this spirit. Prayer is not the language of fear and dread, but of love and confidence. It is not a groaning extorted by the pressure of mere misery, like the howling of wild beasts, to which indeed the Lord likens the petitions of wicked men in their sorrows, where he says: "They have not cried unto me with their hearts, when they howled upon their beds;" Hos. vii. 14: but it is the breathing forth of our wants with an affectionate confidence in him who alone can supply them. The more clearly we realize the character of God as our reconciled Father in Christ, and our relation to him as his children, the more we possess of the element of the spirit of prayer.

An habitual and trustful anticipation of all from God, which he has promised in his word, authorized us to ask, and encouraged us to expect, is another thing essential to this spirit. If God had given us no promises of blessings, no warrant to ask for them, no reason to expect them, prayer, if presented at all, could be offered at best but in painful uncertainty, in gloomy despondency, or in feeble and fluctuating hope. There might by possibility be prayer, but there could not be the spirit of it, which certainly implies a cheerful expectation of being heard, answered, and blessed. Such, then, are the elements of the spirit I am now enjoining, a deep sense of want, and of dependance upon God; a lively faith in God as the hearer and answerer of prayer, and in Christ as the medium; a spirit of adoption, and a trustful expectation of such blessings from God, as are needful for our real welfare. In the absence of these things, however we may abound in the exercises and the forms of devotion, there can be no prayer. These constitute the very soul of all piety toward God, and without which the best composed formularies and the most evangelical sentiments, are but as the statute or the corpse, without the animating mind. These are necessary to all acceptable petitions to God: and the more they are cultivated, the more we shall feel disposed and enabled to pray: these cherished in the heart will make every place an oratory, and produce not merely an occasional, but an abiding intercourse with God.

But another thing intended by the spirit of prayer, is *a scriptural, intelligent, and deep conviction of the necessity, utility, and value of this exercise;* a state of mind the very opposite of that expressed by some of old, who said, " What profit should we have if we pray unto him." Job xxi. 15. The design and utility of prayer are altogether set aside or *attempted* to be set aside by worldly and wicked men, and that by various modes of false reasoning: and even lukewarm Christians are occasionally entangled in the sophisms and fallacies of such infidel objections. But a man in whom lives the *spirit* of prayer, is little troubled with such cavils and difficulties. He not only bows to the authority of God who has enjoined the exercise, but he sees too clearly the evidences of its utility, and has tasted too sweetly its rich advantages to stand in any doubt about the matter. He has proved its direct tendency to improve his character, to lighten his cares, to alleviate his sorrows, to subdue his corruptions, and to obtain the blessings which he needed; and, therefore, by the results of his experience, as well as by the testimony of Scripture, and the consent of the church of God, he has learned to think highly of prayer. It is in him a rooted conviction that it is not a vain thing thus to serve the Lord. He has learned to consider prayer the very soul of godliness, and the life of religion; and forms his estimate of the degree of piety collectively or individually possessed by others, by the degree of prayer to which they have attained. With him a man of piety means a man of prayer; and an eminent Christian is one, in whom is an eminent measure of the gift and grace of prayer.

The spirit of prayer means, *a love to the exercise, and an habitual delight in it.* It is that state of mind, at least resembles it, which in secular matters we call having a *taste* for anything; which in addition to the *performance* of the thing, implies a *delight* in the performing of it; which, though it may refer to a matter of *duty*, converts the doing of it into a *privilege*, and takes off the idea of compulsion, and hardship, and penance. Prayer is the delight of him in whom dwells the spirit of it. The closet is his beloved retreat, to which he is drawn by an attraction, like that which allures us to the society of a beloved and valued friend in his own home when he is alone. He does not go there to perform a penance, quiet his conscience, and get rid of a task which *must* be done, and the sooner it is done the better. No. He loves to go and disburden his mind, and express his wants, and breathe out his desires to God. He loves God, and his prayers are his communings with God. It is to no other than God, supremely good and glorious, and to *his* God by covenant engagement, that his soul elevates herself in prayer—elevates not only her intellect, but her conscience, her affections, her sympathies—her whole immortal and ethereal self; not to speculate, but to adore—to commune—to breathe out his love, and desires, and longings, into the very bosom and heart of the High and Holy One. It is to God through Christ, and by the Spirit's help that he speaks, and opens his lips in ingenuous confession, grateful thanksgiving, adoring praise, and strong supplication; and there also, while prostrate before the flowing fountain of life, he expands his heart to receive the vital streams of light and love, as they gush from their crystal and perennial source. Now this is joy, and peace, and sacred delight.

True it is, that it is not always so. There are seasons when, through the chilling influence of the world, the power of unbelief, and the urgency of care, or the pressure of anxiety, he too much neglects his duty and slights his privilege; but still, just in proportion as the spirit of prayer is possessed by any one, is there a love of prayer — and this love is the spirit of it.

Where this state of mind exists in a high degree, there is, in addition to the habit of prayer at stated seasons, *a prevailing disposition to blend the exercise of it with all the occurrences of life*, and to permeate and season the whole of our character and conduct with its blessed and sanctifying influence. The man in whom it dwells *gives himself to prayer;* surrenders up his mind, and heart, and conscience, and life, to its guiding and controlling power. In one sense he literally "prays always," and "continues instant in prayer." The morning, and evening, and mid-day visit to the throne of grace do not satisfy him; nor even "the seven times a day" calling upon God. His heart, like a round ball which needs but the gentlest impulse to set it in motion, requires only the slightest incident to give it a direction toward God in the act of prayer. Is he going into any new situation of trial and of danger, he runs by prayer to God as his shield and buckler. Does he foresee the coming storm of affliction, he places himself by prayer in the refuge provided. Has some premonition of approaching prosperity been granted him, he anticipates its ensnaring influence by fervent supplication. He thus watches unto prayer, looking around him, and before him, for the circumstances which render it necessary and important. And in addition to this also, he lives in the practice and the confirmed habit of ejaculatory prayer. He seems never to trust himself far from the throne of grace; and walking with God, realizes his presence everywhere. In his house, as he silently surveys his mercies or his trials, he often sends up a short petition for a sanctified use of both; and, when seated amid his children, secretly aspirates the desire: "Oh that Ishmael may live before thee." As he walks along the streets and hears the blasphemies of the profane, and sees the wickedness of the wicked, he darts a petition to heaven for the pouring out of the spirit of God upon the people. While his form moves through the crowd, with no visible or audible sign of devotion, he is walking with God and conversing with heaven. In his transactions with men, he still maintains this intercourse with God. Is he provoked, till he begins to feel his spirit growing hot within him: he suddenly controls his rising anger by the power of prayer. Is he injured; he prays, "Father, forgive them, for they know not what they do." Does a sudden temptation assail his integrity or chastity, or mercy, he sighs forth a supplication for grace to resist it. See him in his attendance upon the means of grace: it is not enough that he prayed for his minister and for himself in his closet before he left the house, but on the way to the sanctuary his thoughts go up in prayer to heaven, for the blessing which his soul needs. He prays while hearing the sermon, and instead of dissipating by frivolous conversation the impressions it has made on his mind, he seals them upon his heart by silent prayer on his way home. In company, he is sometimes in a world of his own, and unheard and unseen, is wrestling with God for some individual present, who needs his intercession, or in reference to some circumstance which the conversation has brought before him. In his silent and solitary walks amid the scenes of nature, he communes with nature's God. When the dispensations of Providence are mentioned in his hearing, whether they refer to the nation at large, or to individuals, or families, he finds a subject of prayer suggested, which gives him an errand to God. The moral and spiritual state of the world is mentioned in his hearing, and instead of putting off the subject till the missionary prayer-meeting comes round, he ejaculates with a sigh the petition: "Let thy way be known upon earth, thy saving health among all nations."

In this way the spirit of prayer diffuses itself throughout the whole character and conduct of him in whom it flourishes. It can no more be confined to times, and places, and particular occasions, than the spirit of patriotism, or of philosophy, or of commerce, can be shut up to periodical exercises and expressions in some special places. No.

when the spirit of any occupation or pursuit be in a man, it will be like a part of himself, and will follow him everywhere, and into everything. And this applies as truly to prayer as to anything else.

You mistake, then, if your only idea of prayer be that of an exercise to be performed night and morning, whether in pre-composed forms, or in extemporaneous expressions, of a given length, a certain vehemence, or a due solemnity, and which being done, is all that is required. Prayer is something more than this, it is the sense of want and of dependance upon God constantly cherished in the soul; habitually leading to expressions of desire, according to his own method of giving utterance to our necessities. Stated times there must and will be for this exercise in the ordinary circumstances of life, and these should be regularly, solemnly, and spiritually observed: but these constitute a very small part of the life of prayer. With too many they are only forms, observed out of mere custom, or to keep the conscience quiet, but carried on in total separation from the living spirit.

The spirit of prayer supposes not only sincerity, and constancy, and an all-pervading exercise, but also *importunity* and *fervor*. It is not merely correct language, and evangelical sentiments, and solemn tones, and reverential postures, but strong desires, ardent aspirations, and importunate entreaties. "It is the effectual *fervent* prayer of the righteous man that availeth much." James v. 16. What specimens of this have we in the Psalms of David. *Those* inspired models of prayer are not mere words, but desires issuing from the inmost recesses of the soul, the groanings of the heart, the struggles of an agonizing spirit, and uttered in appropriate and impassioned language. And what believer has not passed through seasons in which no words of his own seemed sufficiently expressive of his intense feelings; and he has, therefore, had recourse to these cries of the man after God's own heart, as the best outlets of the deep sorrows and ardent wishes of his own laboring soul. By importunity, I do not mean loud and clamorous language, much less rude and unhallowed familiarity, or demand and dictation, but the beseeching spirit, and imploring heart; which in many cases is the groaning that cannot be uttered, and the faith that takes hold of God's strength. How often, after we have listened to some more than ordinary importunate supplication presented at the meetings for social devotion, have we felt and said: "That *was* the very *spirit* of prayer." Yea, we have had, may be, such seasons in our own closet. It was not the flow of words merely, for, perhaps, we could find none sufficiently expressive and emphatic to convey the mighty wants and wishes that were burning in the heart for utterance. No: it was the struggles and wrestling of the laboring breast after some object of its intense desire, and in reference to which it felt almost prompted and authorized to say: "I will not let thee go except thou bless me."

Such, my dear friends, is what I mean by the spirit of prayer. Some of you know it by a blessed experience, far better than I can describe it; but others, I am afraid, know too little about it, and are ready, perhaps, to consider and to call it mere enthusiasm, or the raptures of a mystic piety. You know better, at least most of you, and happy shall I be, if my description of it shall stir you up to cultivate this devotional frame of mind. There is far too little of it in the present day. This fine ethereal temper is but too apt to dissipate amid the bustle and ardor of our stirring age. Blessed be God, it is a stirring age, nor would I paralyze an energy, nor suppress an effort that is employed for the world's conversion. I would not call home the laborer from the great field of Christian zeal, to shut him up in the closet or the cloister of personal devotion; but I would entreat him to make the closet his dwelling-place, *to* which he shall nightly retire to cultivate the spirit of prayer, and *from* which, with a vigorous and healthy piety, he shall go forth in the morning to his holy industry. I want the church to be fitted for her great calling and commission in the conversion of the world, by an appropriate frame and disposition. This kind goeth not forth but by fasting and prayer. Eminent piety is essential to eminent usefulness. It is only in the spirit of faith and prayer that the church can hope to convert the world.

And what is the duty and the business of the church as a whole, is the duty and the business of every one of its members.

Let *every one* enter into this *vital* subject, for such it is. Your spiritual health must be estimated by the measure in which you possess this love and practice of prayer. This is soul prosperity, followed out, as it will be, where it really exists, by all the various details of Christian holiness. The spirit of prayer is the great antagonist of sin. "If I regard iniquity in my heart," said the Psalmist, "the Lord will not hear me." Psalm lxvi. 18. Nothing opposes such a resistance and counteraction to the corruptions of our nature as this frame of mind. The fire of devotion will be in us, if it exist at all, as a purifying fire. And then what a source of comfort would this indwelling spirit of devotion prove to us. It would give us an abiding sense of the nearness of God, and keep us ever walking on the verge of heaven. We could thus converse with God wherever we go. As soon as we retired into ourselves with a design to breathe out our desires to him, we should find him with us. As soon as we think, so soon are we with God. In the twinkling of an eye we find him. We look unto him and are lightened. Thus with a cast of the mind's eye, the soul is filled, and finds itself replenished with a divine and vital light, that diffuseth the sweetest and most pleasant influences through the whole soul. How would it soften the cares, lighten the sorrows, and facilitate the duties of life, if this habitual reference to God pervaded all. How would it smooth our rugged course across this desert earth, thus to draw down upon it the light and the help of Heaven.

Dear friends, know your privilege, and cultivate the spirit of prayer: if this be low, all is low in the soul; while, if this be vigorous, all is vigorous.

> "Prayer makes the darkened cloud withdraw;
> Prayer climbs the ladder Jacob saw;
> Gives exercise to faith and love;
> Brings every blessing from above.
>
> "Restraining prayer we cease to fight;
> Prayer makes the Christian's armor bright;
> And Satan trembles when he sees
> The weakest saint upon his knees."

In the cultivation of the spirit of prayer, it is of great consequence that we recollect our dependance for this, as well as for the right performance of every other branch of Christian duty, is on the aid of the Holy Ghost. The Divine Spirit is our prompter and helper in prayer, as well as the efficient agent in all the other parts of true holiness. "Likewise," says the apostle, "the spirit also helpeth our infirmities, for we know not what we should pray for as we ought: but the spirit itself maketh intercession for us with groanings which cannot be uttered. And he that searcheth the hearts knoweth what is the mind of the spirit, because he maketh intercession for the saints according to the will of God." Rom. viii. 26, 27.

"Praying always with all prayer and supplication in the spirit." Ephes. vi. 18. "But ye, beloved, building up yourselves on your holy faith, praying in the Holy Ghost." Jude 20. In all these passages very explicit reference is made to the work of the spirit in prayer. Not, however, that we are to neglect prayer, any more than we are to neglect any other part of our duty, till we feel a conscious impulse of the Spirit moving us to it; but we are to go continually to the exercise, in a state of desire after and dependance upon this Divine helper of our infirmities. We are not to wait *for* the Spirit, but to work and pray *in* the Spirit. It is the Spirit that gives us a just and impressive view of our wants, that produces, in fact, *all* the elements of prayer; that stirs up the slumbering graces of the soul; that gives clear encouraging views of God as the hearer and answerer of prayer; that assists the believer to understand the word of God, and to take encouraging views of the atonement and intercession of Christ. Consider, then, your need of the Spirit; pray for the Spirit; expect the Spirit; lean upon the Spirit. The spirit of prayer in man is the production of the spirit of God. You need a double intercessor in prayer, so great is this act and exercise; an intercessor for you in heaven, which is Christ; and an intercessor in you upon earth, which is the Holy Spirit; and you have, or may have, both.

Whatever you do in the way of active duty; whatever you give in the way of liberality; what ever you endure in the way of suffering; do not be satisfied with your state, do not conclude that "it is well" with you as a Christian, without much of that frame of mind, which it is the object of this address to explain and recommend; and it will be a rich reward and consolation to me, if I shall see evidence that this effort of your pastor has been blessed to increase in you the spirit of prayer.

No. XI.

PRIVATE PRAYER.

My Dear Friends: "Apostacy from God begins at the closet door." So said the excellent Matthew Henry; and the experience of multitudes has proved the truth of the remark. A prayerless profession of religion will soon be thrown aside as an encumbrance. To guard you against this fearful state, and to lead you on to higher degrees of a devotional enjoyment, is the design of the present number, as well as of the preceding one. The last was on the *spirit* of prayer, without which no religious exercises are either profitable to us, or acceptable to God; and the subject of this admonition is that particular kind of supplication which we denominate *private* prayer, because it is performed by each individual in retirement. This species of devotion is inseparable from a state of grace; it is one of the first, one of the plainest, and strongest symptoms of spiritual life.

A Christian sustains a personal relation to God, has personal wants, sins, and obligations, and feels it therefore both his duty and his privilege to go and speak to God alone. To this he is enjoined by the highest authority: "But thou when thou prayest," said Christ, "enter into thy closet, and when thou hast shut thy door, pray to thy Father which is in secret; and thy Father which seeth in secret, shall reward thee openly." Matt. vi. 6. The word "closet" in the original, signifies chamber, warehouse, or even cellar; in short any secret place: and some suppose our Lord designedly employed a word of such latitude, that none might omit prayer under a pretence that they had not a proper place to which to retire. Place is nothing, disposition in prayer is everything. "I will," said the apostle, "that men pray *everywhere*, lifting up holy hands." Blessed privilege! There is no place in which it is suitable for a Christian to be found, in which it is unsuitable for him to pray.

Nothing is said in Scriptures either as to the time, the frequency, or the length of our prayers. Nature seems to point out, as suitable, the morning, when we are going forth to meet the duties and dangers, trials and difficulties of the world; and the evening, when we have to review the conduct of the day, and need protection for the night. And how beneficial have many found five or ten minutes at noon given to this sacred exercise. A solemn, though it be a *short* pause at mid-day to send up a look to God, a cry to heaven, would prove a sweet refreshment, and a powerful protection. No general rule can be laid down as to the *length* of our private devotions. This, like many other of our duties under the Christian dispensation, is intrusted to our sense of duty, and to our feelings of love and gratitude. It depends in measure on the nature and number of other duties; the peculiarity of our situation; the specific objects for which we pray; the engagedness of our attention; and the intensity of our feelings. Colonel GARDINER, whose engagements were such that he could often command only one season of retirement in a day, used to spend two hours in devotion before he went out in a morning; to command which he always rose early, and if it were necessary, as was sometimes the case, when his regiment was on the march, for him to leave home before the time allotted to his closet, he would rise at an earlier hour to secure his usual term of communion with God. LUTHER thought three hours a day little enough to spend in prayer. Few Christians can imitate these men. Perhaps there are few, who if they had much of the spirit of prayer, could not and would not command half an hour once a day, and most, by a proper economy of time, and an abridgment of unnecessary slumber, could secure double this portion. There is very little danger in these days of feeble devotion, engrossing secularity, and active zeal, of spending too much time in the closet; the danger lies on the other side. Everything connected with religion, except public meetings, which often have very little of religion in them, must be short—short sermons—short prayers—short meditations—short devotion—short books—short religion.

It does not much matter *what* part of the day is devoted to prayer. No hour is canonical. Most persons find it convenient to give the morning before the business of the world commences, and the evening, after it is finished but some, for instance, servants and laboring men, and the mothers of young families, cannot so exactly and independently command and arrange their time, and they must get what they can, and select the time most convenient to their peculiar circumstances. Deeply do I feel for these classes of my members, and most anxious am I, lest in the urgency of their pursuits, the constant recurrence of their duties, and the wearisome nature of their labors, they should lose the spirit and love of prayer, by being deprived of much of the opportunity for its periodical and regular performance; and sink into a state of lukewarmness and neglect. Endeavor, my dear friends, to keep up *habitual* devotion in your souls; and as intervals of leisure can be found through the day, steal away to your chamber at any hour to commune with God in secret. In this respect "watch unto prayer," by looking after those opportunities which you may be able to embrace without neglecting other incumbent duties.

Perhaps a few DIRECTIONS for the right performance of this exercise, may be of importance. *Do not be satisfied with mere formality.* Forget not you have to do with one who searcheth the heart and trieth the reins of the children of men. How indignantly did God complain of the Jews when he said: "This people draweth nigh unto me with their mouth, and honoreth me with their lips, but their heart is far from me." Matt. xv. 8. Nothing is more insulting to God, or more injurious to ourselves, than cold, heartless, formal prayers. Our devotions do us either great good or harm. Insincere and spiritless prayers are a most profane trifling with religion; they are like offering dead sacrifices upon God's altar which are not only unacceptable to him, but harden the hearts of those by whom they are presented. Some persons are made worse by their very devotions. Nothing tends more to abate our reverence for God, or our fear of offending him, than a careless method of addressing him. The servant that can habitually speak to his master in a disrespectful manner, acquires a familiarity, which saps the very principle of obedience. Be solemn then and devout in all your addresses to God, for he is a *jealous* God.

Let your prayers be strictly private. "Enter into thy closet, and *shut thy door;* pray to thy Father which is *in secret.*" There should not be a single human being, with you: the presence even of a child, capable of noticing what is going on, should be felt as a hinderance, a restraint, and an embarrassment. It is not enough, that only your husband, or your wife, is with you; even this near and dear friend must be away. You must be alone with God. If prayer were a mere form, this entire privacy would not be necessary; but it is a spiritual exercise; it is the breathing out of the heart to God; it is the mind disburdening herself to God; it is the soul in the confessional with God, where there are sins to be confessed, sorrows to be uttered, petitions to be presented, and thanksgivings to be offered which no ear but his must hear, or ought to hear. It is true, there may be cases in which this absolute privacy, at least for a constancy, is difficult, if not impossible; and in this case, a very rare one, I admit, it is better to pray before others, than not at all. But who cannot be sometimes alone? Even where two or more sleep in the same room, that same room is not always engaged, and may be occupied some part of the day by the lover of prayer. Those who content themselves with merely dropping upon their knees and repeating a few words, on retiring to rest, or rising in the morning, before others, but who never seek to be alone; who have no desire for devotion, strictly secret; who have nothing to say to God, which he alone must listen to, and feel no impulse to speak to him, when no one is by, know nothing of prayer: they may maintain the form, but they know nothing of the power of godliness. The saints of Scripture are represented as going to pray apai ISAAC went by himself to the fields to meditate, and doubtless to pray. JACOB wrestled alone with the angel at Peniel. MOSES worshipped alone at the burning bush DAVID's Psalms were most of them prayers, uttered in absolute retirement. DANIEL prayed in his chamber alone. PHILIP lifted up his heart under the fig-tree. PETER went up to the house-top to pray. Yea, our divine LORD went often by himself into a mountain to pray.

Our prayers ought to be specific, varied, and definite. We should not go to the throne of the heavenly majesty without an errand and an object. Many people go away into their closets because they must say their prayers. The time has come when they are in the habit of going by themselves for prayer in the morning, at noon, or whatever time of the day it may be; and instead of having anything to say, any definite object before the mind, they fall down on their knees, and pray for just what comes into their minds; for everything that floats in their imaginations at the time, and when they have done, they could hardly tell a word of what they had been praying for. This is not effectual prayer. What should we think of anybody who should try to move a legislature so, and should say: "Now it is winter, and the parliament is sitting, and it is time to send up petitions;" and should go up to the legislature and petition at random, without any definite object? Do you think such petitions would move the legislature? Many people's prayers are nothing else but this going into their room, and saying just what comes into their heads at the time, and hence if they do not use a form, as few do or need, their prayers are mere incoherent words, or ramblings of thought, which have scarcely the character of prayer about them; and which, if they were penned down, and shown to them afterward, would cause them to blush that they had ever thus addressed the great and holy God. To guard against this, it would be well to have a list of subjects of prayer, either in the mind, or drawn up on paper, and one appropriated to each day. The orderly returns of days and nights invite us to this: there seem to be subjects which belong to particular seasons; Saturday evening calls us to confession of sin, and thanksgiving for mercies: sabbath morning to prayer for ministerial holiness, and success in preaching the word: Monday morning to ask for help in duty, and grace to adorn our profession in all the various obligations of social and civil life. Thus each day might have its appropriated subject of prayer, and object of specific errand to the throne of God. One day may be specially appointed for thanksgiving, another for adoration, another for petition. One may be set apart for our relatives, another for those who desire an interest in our supplications. All the great Christian institutions of the age; our own religious denomination; the holy catholic church; our country; may all, and should all, be introduced, not for mere form's sake, or cursorily and as by accident, but specifically, successively, with a deep interest in their welfare and a devout recollection that God alone can bless them. As your teacher and pastor, I say to you: "Brethren, pray for me." I need your prayers. I ask them. I am entitled to them. I value them. Remember me in your holiest moments, and nearest approaches to God. And do not forget your fellow-members. Let your church have a large share of your private prayers.

There are many advantages in this. Such a method would lead us *actually* to pray, whereas a great deal of what goes by that name does not deserve to be so called; it would keep our thoughts from wandering, a subject of incessant complaint with most Christians; it would render the exercise more interesting, by giving us an object, and keeping up variety; and it would engage our hearts in a more solemn and sacred manner in the various matters which are thus successively carried by us to the footstool of heaven. This plan of select subjects for prayer has been tried by many persons with vast advantage to the devotional state of their souls. It is not necessary the list of subjects should be fixed and invariable, but be sometimes changed; yet still, ever presenting something definite to the mind in her approaches to God. Some new object will be ever supplying itself to the Christian in the course of his reading, observation, or experience, which, while it constantly becomes the subject of a momentary ejaculation to God at the time, may be treasured up in his mind, for more specific and lengthened supplication at a convenient season.

Such a prayer; the feeling of a strong desire after some definite object, relating either to ourselves or others, which we know God alone can grant, and which, therefore, we carry to him in the way of fervent and believing supplication. It is the expression to him of something we really feel at the time, either of gratitude, adoration, humiliation, or petition, and to express which we enter our closet, and shut the door to commune about this very matter with our Father which seeth in secret.

But if you should not deem it best, or necessary, to keep a list of subjects, and to appropriate them to particular days, still, in every approach to God in prayer, let there be a solemn pause, while the inquiry is asked: "What should I now make the subject of my petition at the throne of grace?" The mind would then have some object on which to concentrate its thoughts and feelings. There is a danger, as I have, I believe, expressed before in a former number, lest the frequency and constant recurrence of the seasons of devotion, should abate in our minds that seriousness and deliberation with which we ought ever to call upon the Lord; and thus the whole business of prayer would sink into a mere form.

Connect with private prayer, the perusal of the Word of God, meditation, self-examination, and, where there is time for it, the reading of devotional uninspired books, especially religious biography: but as there is with many Christians but a limited opportunity for reading, and no book should be allowed to supplant the Bible, it is best to allot the few minutes that can be spared for this exercise, to the Word of God. Read this, not promiscuously, but in regular course. Do not waste your time in inquiring what portion you should read, "much less adopt the heathenish practice of dipping into the Bible, as a lottery book, to try your luck in finding suitable passages."

It is obvious that if a Christian would keep up the exercise of the closet with edification and enjoyment, *he must make a solemn business of it.* The whole matter must be one of conscience, and of vast importance. *He must find time for it*, and if his heart be right with God, he *will.* He will watch unto prayer. It will be matter of contrivance with him to guard against whatever would prevent, or shorten his exercises; it will be a grief to him to be interrupted; and in order to have time at command for the exercise, he will rise early for this purpose. *Perhaps there is not a more common or successful hinderance to private prayer than late rising from bed.* How many slumber away, I repeat it, that time in bed which should be spent in supplication to God. Tell me not you have no time to pray, if you have made up your mind to lie sleeping till eight o'clock in the morning. If you cannot sacrifice half an hour's ease to commune with God, to attend to your soul's concerns, to prepare by devotion for the trials and duties of the day, what is your religion worth? How can you be in earnest? How can you expect your soul to prosper?

But there is another direction I would give,

and that is, in addition to the usual and regular seasons of prayer, *set apart occasional and extraordinary ones*, when, with more than ordinary solemnity and length, you enter into the concerns of your soul; and it would be well also to unite *fasting* with prayer. Such seasons, devoutly observed, have wonderful power to check the growth of worldly-mindedness, to rouse the flagging spirit of devotion, to increase spirituality, subdue irregularities, and to cast out every unclean spirit from the mind. They invigorate every Christian purpose, move the deep fountains of spiritual feeling, launch our spirits on the ocean of eternity, and lead us to commune with its transforming realities. MARTIN LUTHER devoted one day every week in this way, and far from finding it tedious, he hailed it as the best of the six. I do not say that many can imitate him in the *extent* of his practice, but all may in the *principle* of it. Set apart such seasons, as your birthday, your new-birth day, if it can be ascertained, the last day of the year, or the anniversary of some signal deliverance, or an occasional sabbath evening after the Lord's Supper, as a season of special prayer.

I will now correct a few MISTAKES into which some have fallen on the subject of private prayer.

The closet ought not to be considered, as it is by many, *exclusively devoted to our own personal religion*. Private prayer is not to be made selfish prayer. Our own wants, woes, sins, and duties, are *one* object, and indeed the *primary* one, but not the only one. We should be happier and holier than we are, if we had more love to others, more feeling for the church and the world, and less of *individual* feeling. Charity and brotherly-kindness, did they exist as they ought, would overflow from the heart in intercession for their proper objects, at those seasons when we were praying for ourselves.

Christians oftentimes *do not pray in faith:* and yet this is prescribed, and prescribed too, as the condition of success. James i. 6. To pray in faith means a firm persuasion that through the mediation of Christ, we are authorized to pray; that our prayers are really heard; and that in spiritual blessings, we shall have *the very* things we ask; and in temporal ones, *those* or *better*. Many persons do not care about success through carelessness, others do not expect it, through despondency: but faith after looking *up* for the blessing, actually looks *out* for it. Effectual prayer is not mere clamorous importunity, but believing expectation. We must not knock at the door of mercy, and then walk away in despair, but wait in hope.

We must not allow family prayer to supersede that which is private and personal; any more than we should allow public worship to supersede the sacrifice at the family altar. It is an ill sign for any one who feels a disposition to make attention to one duty an excuse for neglecting another.

Many think they ought not to pray, except they are in a good frame, and feel a strong impulse to the exercise. Our feelings cannot be the standard of our duty. If we adopt the rule of never praying except when we feel strongly inclined to it, Satan and a deceitful heart will allow us but few opportunities. We might as well neglect public, social, or domestic worship, because we are not in a good frame, or do not feel the Spirit moving us, as omit private prayer: nay, we might, for the same reason, as well give up reading the Scriptures, and every duty we owe to God or man, till we are *inclined* to them. The very want of disposition is a sin, which we should go and confess to God, and beg for his grace to warm our cold hearts. The *spirit* of prayer, comes to us in the *act* of prayer, and not in the neglect of it. I have read of a Christian female who was induced to act on this unscriptural rule, of praying only when the spirit moved her to it, and she became the prey and sport of temptation, and was for a long time in a state of the most distressing gloom and doubts of her piety.

Some I am afraid are putting the regular performance of private prayer in the place of other duties, and making it a substitute for other and more self-denying parts of religion. There are not a few, who as regularly go into their closet to pray as the time comes round, and who would not be happy to neglect a single opportunity, but whose predominant love of the world, covetousness, bad temper, or other inconsistencies of conduct, plainly indicate a total want of true faith.

Do you need MOTIVES to induce a more earnest attention to the exercise? How many are at hand?

It is not only your incumbent duty, but *the test of the sincerity of your profession.* It you do not practise, and love the exercises of the closet, and make provision for attending to them, you cannot be a Christian. There never yet was a child of God, that did not love to be alone with his Father, and pray to *him in secret.*

What *an honor* is it to be admitted to a private audience with God; to be closeted with the King of kings! A subject feels it to be a distinction to be introduced at court on a levee day, though at such a time, and amid the multitude, he can expect no special attention; but how much richer is the privilege to have an interview and conference with the monarch alone, and there present his petitions, when he has the royal ear to himself!

What *a rich reward does the duty yield when rightly performed.* How precious is the privilege. To have all restraint removed, and feel that we are at freedom to pour out the utmost secrets of our hearts, whether of sin, sorrow, or anxiety. You *must* know this by experience, and how often you have relieved your burdened spirit of its load in that retreat, where neither eye nor ear of man could follow you. Read the biographies of eminent Christians, and there learn the value and the sweetness of private prayer. "I would not," says a lady in her diary, "be hired out of my closet for a thousand worlds. I never enjoy such hours of pleasure, and such free and entire communion with God as I have here; and I wonder that any can live prayerless, and deprive themselves of the greatest privilege allowed them."—"In prayer," says HENRY MARTYN, "I had a most precious view of Christ, as a friend that sticketh closer than a brother! I hardly know how to contemplate with praise enough his adorable excellences. Who can show forth all his praise? I can conceive it to be a theme long enough for eternity. I want no other happiness, no other sort of heaven." BRAINERD in his journal records: "I spent an hour in prayer with great intenseness and freedom, and with the most soft and tender affection toward mankind. O it is an emblem of heaven to love all the world, with a love of kindness, forgiveness, and benevolence. My soul was sweetly resigned to God's disposal of me—I confided in him that he would never leave me, though I should walk through the valley of the shadow of death." How often did Dr. PAYSON write in his journal: "Had a sweet season of prayer this morning, and felt fervent love to my Savior, and desires that he might be glorified." But why should I multiply examples, or refer you to others. If you are Christians as well as professors, your own experience, I repeat, confirms the privilege of prayer. Some of your happiest, holiest seasons on earth have been spent in your closets. There you have communed with God; there your cares have been lightened, your sorrows alleviated, your fears dissipated, and your souls invigorated. There you have conquered the world, subdued your foes, mortified your corruptions. O what hours you have spent, what discoveries you have made, what joys you have experienced!

Think *what an influence secret prayer has upon your whole spirit, and temper, and conduct.* "God's morning smiles bless all the day." Account for it as you may, I believe the fact is unquestionable—that private prayer so regulates and tranquillizes the mind, gives it such a balance, self-possession, and reliance on divine aid, that it happily fits a person for the performance of his most common duties, and enables him to accomplish more, and do it better than he otherwise could. What but prayer gave NEHEMIAH such firmness in building the walls of Jerusalem amid insults and opposition? What else enabled DANIEL to brave the lion's den? Sir MATTHEW HALE, that upright judge, in his letters to his children, says: "If I omit praying and reading a portion of God's blessed word in the morning, nothing goes well with me all the day." BOERHAVE, the celebrated Dutch physician, said, that "his daily practice of retiring for an hour in the morning, and spending it in devotion and meditation, gave him firmness and vigor for the whole day." Dr. DODDRIDGE used frequently to observe, that "he never advanced well in human learning without prayer; and that he always made the most proficiency in his studies when he prayed with the greatest fervency." LUTHER had written on his study door: "To have prayed well, is to have studied well." And is not all this accordant, my dear friends, with your own experience?

What *examples*, then, recommend this practice! But what are these to the example of CHRIST? He also was not only a man of sorrows, but a man of prayers;—

> "Cold mountains and the midnight air
> Witnessed the fervor of his prayer."

And can you have the mind of Christ, and be partakers of his spirit, if there be no love to prayer?

Permit me, then, in conclusion, to ask you, my dear friends, with all the fidelity and affection that belong to my office as your pastor, are you in the habit and love of private prayer? Have you stated and regular times for this duty, and do you keep them? Are you suffering the cares of a family, the engagements of business, or the pursuits of labor, to interfere with this exercise? Have you special seasons for prayer? Do you enjoy the devotions of the closet? Have you the *spirit* of prayer? Have you ceased to pray? If so. Why? Is it the indulgence of sin, the pleasures of the world, or some mistaken view of duty? Oh! do examine. The soul that is neglecting private prayer is in an awful state of backsliding from God. Are you, in such a state, *happy?* Are you ready for death, meet for heaven? Can you be willing to have it recorded against you in the book of God's remembrance: "This is the man that once bowed unto me in his closet; asked for pardoning mercy; that once sued for an interest in his Savior's love; but afterward shut, no more to open, his closet door; broke his most solemn vows; committed again the sins for the pardon of which he prayed, and turned away from the Savior." Oh! my dear friends, return, return speedily to prayer!

No. XII.

SELF-EXAMINATION.

My Dear Friends: This address will reach you at the close of one year, or the beginning of another: in either case its congratulations and directions, its admonitions and cautions, will be in season. Bless the God of your mercies that he has guided, protected, sustained, and supplied you during another year of your pilgrimage in the wilderness state. Raise your Ebenezer, and inscribe upon it: "Hitherto the Lord hath helped me;" and having given utterance to the fulness of a grateful heart, that you are "the living, the living to praise God," proceed to the work of self-examination. One use we should make of the end of our years, is to consider them as resting-places on the hill of life, or stages in its journey, where we should pause, turn round, take out our map, and inquire whether we are in the right road, and what progress we are making. Another year is opening before you with all its unknown unimagined scenes; it may be your last; and *will be* to some of you. Could you read the book of destiny, you would find, perhaps, written opposite your name: "*This year thou shalt die.*" It is, therefore, a suitable admonition to address to you:

"*Set thy house in order, for thou shalt die and not live.*'—" For he that will die well and happily, must dress his soul by a diligent and frequent scrutiny; he must in this world love tears, humility, solitude, and repentance."

SELF-EXAMINATION is a duty enjoined upon us both by reason and Scripture. Observe with what vehemence the apostle enforces it: "Examine yourselves whether ye be in the faith; prove your own selves; know ye not your own selves, that Jesus Christ is in you except ye be reprobates." 2 Cor. xiii. 5. This, recollect, was addressed to professing Christians, and is an exercise in which all *true* believers have ever practised themselves. No one can be really in earnest about the salvation of his soul, who never looks with solicitude into his spiritual state.

There are two ends for which this duty is to be performed—first, to ascertain the *sincerity and reality* of our religion; and, secondly, its *condition:* in other words, to inquire whether we be *in the faith,* and also in what degree we are bringing forth, or neglecting to bring forth, *its fruits:* analogous to what takes place in the conduct of the careful tradesman, who inspects his affairs to find out, in the first place, whether he is solvent; and in the next, what is the amount of his profits, and how, by avoiding past errors, or making up discovered deficiencies, he can increase his prosperity. So a diligent, watchful, careful professor, is anxious to know not only that he *is* a Christian, but how his religion can be improved and increased. It is true, some are happily partakers of so large a measure of the well-founded assurance of faith and hope, as to have few doubts about their state; and, indeed, little cause for them. They have so much of the spirit of adoption, as constantly to enjoy the witness of the Spirit of God, that they are his children. It is not so, however, with *all* Christians, and even those with whom it is, may occasionally examine with profit, the state of their souls, if it be only to increase their confidence in the reasons of the hope that is in them.

How momentous is the question: "Am I really a child of God!" What consequences hang upon the decision of such a matter! The very possibility of self-deception here, is truly horrifying To wake up from the sleep of death in hell instead of heaven, and find that we have made a mistake which requires an eternity fully to understand, and an eternity adequately to deplore! Such a mistake *is* made, it is to be feared, by multitudes in every age. And when we consider the deceitfulness of our hearts, our proneness to self-love, and the easiness of making a profession in this tranquil age of the church, there is such imminent peril of a fatal error in our own case, as should send us all to our closets, our hearts, our Bible, and our God, to examine whether *we* "be in the faith." It is a matter which none should take for granted.

If we examine ourselves, it must be by som

rule, and the only one of any authority in this case is the word of God. The Holy Scriptures are the only touchstone which God will acknowledge. These are the balances of the sanctuary; the legal standard in the assay office of heaven; all that will not stand this test must be thrown aside, as reprobate silver. To the law and the testimony, then, must be our appeal. Our faith must be tested by the gospel; our practice by the law; and our spirit and temper by the mind of Christ. He is the model, the pattern, the measure by which all his followers are to be examined, for both law and gospel are imbodied in him.

I will now lay down some rules and considerations and cautions by which this important business must be carried on.

1. Do not examine yourselves only by your own notion of what a Christian is and should be, and be satisfied if you come up to that, because that notion may itself be wrong. Many frame to themselves an exceedingly inaccurate idea of what is included in religion; and yet if they possess this, are quite contented. This is what the apostle calls, "comparing themselves with themselves," and has led in innumerable cases to self-delusion and self-destruction. Before you are satisfied, then, with the conclusion that you answer to your own idea of a Christian, take good care to examine by the Bible whether that idea itself be a scriptural one.

2. Do not examine yourselves merely by the

creeds and catechisms, the formularies, rites, and ceremonies of any particular church; or by the sentiments, opinions, and criteria, of any individual uninspired writer; nor be satisfied if you imagine you come up to these standards. Such tests need themselves to be tried, for they are all fallible. The Bible, the Bible alone is the religion of Christians. Uninspired works may be used with advantage, as helps, but not as infallible standards.*

3. Do not be satisfied with the good opinion of others upon your state. Some persons are too prone to get rid of their fears and take refuge in the favorable estimate formed of their piety by those who rank high in their view for judgment and experience. It is more safe, in some cases, to regard the sentiments of those who are prejudiced against us. Your friends cannot see your heart. Their kindness to you and affection for you, may lead them to form the best opinion they can, and their love to you may make them blind to defects which are incompatible with sincere piety, or at any rate, with that which is eminent. Besides, their own religion may be so defective and inconsistent, as to give easy credence, for their own sakes, to the reality of yours. Do not be flattered

* I here recommend an exceedingly valuable little work, entitled, "Am I a Christian, or Aids to Self-Examination," by the Rev. HUBBARD WINSLOW. It contains the celebrated "resolutions" of JONATHAN EDWARDS and rules for "Growth in Grace"

into self-deception. Let not their ignorant and injudicious adulation stand between you and the Bible; it is what this says, and not what your friends say that must determine your state.

4. Do not consider that all is right because you are admitted to membership upon the examination of a minister, or even that of a church in addition, and conclude that your Christianity is sincere because your profession has been admitted to be credible. *There is a path leading from the sacramental table, trodden by thousands, to the bottomless pit!*

5. Beware of judging of yourselves, by partial and detached views of your conduct. To this we are extremely prone. Ever ready to depart from universal regard to the ways of God, we are disposed to rest on some one action or set of actions, as an evidence that all is well with us, and flatter ourselves on this ground, that we are the servants of Jehovah. It is conceivable that many may be prone from taste, situation, interest, or other circumstances to some one branch of Christian duty, who are lamentably remiss in others, the obligations of which though equally strong and plain, are unfelt and resisted. Self-examination must embrace the whole of the divine law, and the whole of our character. We must examine whether we possess that love to God and holiness which is the principle of all right obedience, and which if it *be* possessed, makes us willing and anxious to do the whole will of God.

6. Do not in default of present evidence, go back to past experience, and coupling this with perverted views of the doctrine of the perseverance of the saints, conclude that you are Christians, although there be no satisfactory existing proofs of faith and godliness. When the conclusion is drawn from past, instead of present evidence, and the awakened conscience is hushed again to slumber by the opiate of such a sentiment as that, once a child of God, a child of God for ever, the delusion is awful, and the consequences are likely to be dreadful and eternal.

7. Do not take up the business of self-examination in order to quiet a conscience, feeling the burden of its guilt, and to free the soul from painful apprehensions of the wrath of God. If you have not known the gospel scheme of salvation by grace, and justification by faith; or having known it, have fallen into sin, and thus lost the peace and comfort of your mind, your duty, and the way to quietness and assurance, is not to set about looking into your heart, and back upon your past conduct, to find out evidences of a state of grace; nor to seek the judgment of others, who in ignorance or in kindness, may endeavor to lull your solicitude and flatter you into a good opinion of your state, by reminding you of former zeal, and telling you that God often in sovereignty withdraws from his people because they cannot bea uninterrupted comfort;—but instead of this, tc apply at once by faith to the blood of Christ tha

cleanseth from all sin. You are to be directed to the cross, and to be required to believe the testimony that Christ will cast out none that come unto him If this does not relieve you, God has provided no other ground of comfort, and you ought to beware of seeking any other either from yourselves or from your friends. Self-examination is never to be put in place of the exercise of faith; nor is it intended or calculated to give relief to the burdened sinner, or to restore the comfort of a trembling backslider. A person in either of these states of mind, may gain a short and fitful repose from the supposition that self-scrutiny has disclosed something in their favor, but it is a delusive, and will be likely to be a transient quietude, and like that produced by opiates for the body, it will soon pass of, and leave the spirit more restless and wretched than ever.

8. Do not be satisfied with a conclusion that rests upon the lowest possible degree of evidence in your favor. Our faith is susceptible of various degrees of strength, and its fruits may be brought forth in greater or less abundance. It is a fearful problem for any man to attempt to solve, to try with how little religion he may be a real Christian, and go to heaven. Do not compose yourselves to sleep with the idea, that though you are not so eminent as some others, and even have many glaring defects and inconsistences, you are right in the main. It may be so; for weak faith, is sincere faith; and little grace, real grace; but

how difficult is it for us to determine, when faith is so weak, and grace is so feeble, that they exist at all! Christ hath said: "Herein is my Father glorified that ye bear much fruit. So shall ye be my disciples." John xv. 8. If then the test of discipleship be *much* fruit, it is unsafe to rest our conclusion upon *a little*. The more we are conformed to the image of Christ, and the more we have of the mind that was in him, the more decisive is the evidence that we are in the faith. O who that is in any degree alive to the importance of salvation, and to the blessedness of an assured hope of it, will be content with those low degrees of evidence, which leave their possessors ever fluctuating between hope and fear?

9. Enter upon the work of examination with the double purpose of increasing both your joy, and your holiness. Religious comfort, joy, and peace in believing, are of immense consequence, not only to your happiness, but your safety. "The joy of the Lord is your strength." Neh. viii. 10. "The peace of God which passeth all understanding keepeth your hearts and minds through Jesus Christ." Phil. iv. 7. Religious joy makes duty cheerful, trials light, temptations powerless, and worldly amusements insipid. It is of importance therefore to increase it; and the self-examination of real Christians, by revealing the evidence of their sincere belief, produces this increase of the joy of faith. But where *this* end is not answered, and disclosures are made, calculated to

produce an opposite effect, *holiness* may be promoted; for it is never to be forgotten that improvement is one great end of self-scrutiny. He that examines the state of his heart and life at the conclusion of one year, ought to do it with a view to correct what is wrong, and supply what is wanting, during the next.

10. No one should be satisfied with *his own* self-inspection, but by earnest and believing prayer, should entreat of *God* to search him also, and to make known to him his real condition. That man knows not the deceitfulness of his heart, nor is he duly impressed with the danger and consequences of self-deception, who does not occasionally with intense solicitude, present the prayer of the Psalmist: "Search me, O God, and know my heart; try me and know my thoughts, and see if there be any wicked way in me, and lead me in the way everlasting." Psalm cxxxix. 23, 24.

Ask, then, afresh, and with deep solemnity at the close of the present, or at the beginning of the next year, the momentous question: "*Am I a sincere Christian, or only a professor?*" Set apart an additional hour, to inquire into this great subject. O what are all other questions compared with this, but as the small dust of the balance? By all the value you bear for your soul, or your soul's salvation, I entreat you in the most solemn manner, to take up this matter, and spread it before the Lord in prayer. Take the following questions as a test:—

Have you a consciousness that you really believe in Jesus Christ, and are depending upon him, and him alone, for salvation? 1 John v. 10.

Do you bring forth the fruits of faith, which are the fruits of the Spirit, as set before us by the apostle? Gal. v. 6, 22–25. Acts xv. 9. 1 John ii. 15; v. 4.

Do you love God supremely, practically, habitually? 1 John v. 1–3.

Do you love the children of God, for God's sake? 1 John iii. 14.

Are you complying with the apostle's direction in 2 Peter i. 5–10? On what principles do you act, those of the world or of the Bible? What is your predominant object, time or eternity, the world or salvation? 1 Cor. iv. 18. Do you deny yourself for Christ's sake, or are you seeking only self-gratification? Matt. xvi. 25, 26.

How do you employ your talents of property, intellect, influence? For God or self? Rom. xiv. 7–9. 1 Cor. vi. 20. Phil. i. 21.

How do you bear your afflictions? With submission or repining? Rom. v. 3.

For a more minute and lengthened test of religious character, I refer you to my work, entitled, "The Christian Professor," where, in the chapter on "The Self-deceived Professor," you will find much to direct and caution you.

But I will now suppose *the great question* settled, and that you have no serious reason to doubt that you are "in the faith;" still you have to examine into the degree and state of your religion: for it may be very defective, where it is real. In what condition then are you come to the close of the year? You were exhorted at the commencement of it, to make it a year of improvement, and great increase of holiness. Have you done so? Has the exhortation of your pastor been complied with? Have you sought and obtained an increased effusion of divine influence? Has the heavenly shower come down in its season? Have the dispensations of Providence, both in a way of judgment and mercy, been sanctified? Have you improved well your sabbaths, fifty-two more of which have been numbered to you? Where is the fruit of all the sermons you have heard? What are you the better for the renewed culture you have enjoyed? I dare challenge you, and ask you if I have remitted aught of my labor, fidelity, and anxiety for your welfare. Yea, have I not added to it? Have I sought to please you or to PROFIT you? Have I shunned to declare to you the whole counsel of God? Am I not clear from the blood of all of you, if unhappily you should perish?

Well, my dear friends, examine your conduct during the past year. Inquire how you have sustained your various relations, and have discharged your various duties. Masters and mistresses, have you been kind to your servants, just as to their wages, watchful over their souls? Servants, have you been honest, diligent, obedient, respectful, devoted? Fathers, have you kept up family religion with punctuality, seriousness, and affection, being careful of the spiritual welfare of your children? Children, have you been obedient, loving, dutiful? Tradesmen, have you been just, generous, true, faithful to your covenants, and considerate of your work-people? Ye rich, have ye been liberal, humble, heavenly? Ye poor, have ye been contented, submissive, trustful? Ye aged, have ye been cheerful, weaned from the world, communicative to the young? Ye young, have ye been modest, active, useful? As professors, have you been careful to avoid little sins, to maintain a tender and enlightened conscience, a brotherly feeling, and a spirit of charity? All these topics should become matter of self-examination: here is a wide field of inquiry; traverse it all. You must come behind in no duty, but go on unto perfection.

Think not, however, that self-examination is only an *occasional* duty. It should precede every approach to the Lord's table: "Let a man examine himself," says the apostle, "and so let him eat." It should be interwoven with all our reading of the Scriptures, and hearing of the gospel; and, indeed, with the whole series of our actions. It should be a nightly exercise at the close of each day. PYTHAGORAS, a heathen philosopher, said to his disciples: "Let not sleep seize upon your senses before you have three times recalled the conversation and accidents of the day." SENECA, another pagan, said: "At night, when the light is removed, and all is hushed and still, I make a scrutiny into the day, and hide nothing from myself." And now hear the language of a Christian bishop, on the necessity of this evening exercise: "If we consider the disorders of every day—the multitude of idle worlds; the great portions of time spent in vanity; the daily omissions of duty; the coldness of our prayers; the indifferences of our spirit in holy things; the uncertainty of our secret purposes; our deceptions and hypocrisies sometimes not known, very often not observed by ourselves; our want of charity; our not knowing in how many degrees of action and purpose every virtue is to be exercised; the secret adherances of pride, and too forward complacency in our best actions; our failings in all our relations; the niceties of difference between some virtues and some vices; the secret undiscernible passages from lawful to unlawful in the first instances of change; the perpetual mistakings of permission for duty, and licentious practices for permission; our daily abusing the liberty God gives us; our unsuspected sins in managing a life certainly lawful; our little greedinesses in eating, and surprises in the proportions of our drinkings; our too great freedoms and fondnesses in lawful loves; our aptness for things sensual, and our deadness and weariness of spirit in spiritual employments; beside an infinite variety of cases of conscience that do occur in the life of every man, and in all intercourses cf every life—then shall we find that the productions of sin are incredibly numerous and increasing, and the computations of a man's life intricate and almost inexplicable; and, therefore, it is but reason we should sum up our accounts at the foot of every page: I mean that we call ourselves to scrutiny every night, when we compose ourselves to the little images of death."

By this frequent examination, we shall prevent little sins from growing into great ones, and acts from becoming habits; we shall stop the accumulation of those minor transgressions, which, if they do not become greater ones, diminish the lustre of our profession, interrupt our peace, and prey upon our spiritual strength; we shall increase the tenderness of our conscience, promote our watchfulness, make our confession minute, our repentance particular, and greatly advance our holiness.

And now, dear brethren, "yield yourselves to God" afresh at the commencement of another year, "as those that are alive from the dead, and your members as instruments of righteousness unto God."—"I beseech you by the mercies of God, that ye present your bodies a living sacrifice, holy, acceptable unto God, which is your reasonable service; and be not conformed to this world, but be ye transformed by the renewing of your mind, that ye may prove what is that good, that acceptable and perfect will of God." Rom. xii. 1, 2. "As strangers and pilgrims, abstain from fleshly lusts, which war against the soul." 1 Pet.

n. 12. "Pass the time of your sojourning here in fear, forasmuch as ye know ye were not redeemed with corruptible things as silver and gold, but with the precious blood of Christ, as of a lamb without blemish and without spot." 1 Pet. i. 17–19.

Resolve, by God's grace, this shall be the holiest year, and the most useful one, of your whole life; then will it be the happiest; and even though it should be the last, it will be to your emancipated spirit as the year of release, of jubilee, and eternal salvation.

THE END.

www.ingramcontent.com/pod-product-compliance
Lightning Source LLC
LaVergne TN
LVHW011210110826
845150LV00006B/1391

* 9 7 8 1 4 2 5 5 1 7 8 0 9 *